Fisher Investments
on Emerging Markets

FISHER INVESTMENTS PRESS

Fisher Investments Press brings the research, analysis, and market intelligence of Fisher Investments' research team, headed by CEO and *New York Times* best-selling author Ken Fisher, to all investors. The Press covers a range of investing and market-related topics for a wide audience—from novices to enthusiasts to professionals.

Books by Ken Fisher
How to Smell a Rat
The Ten Roads to Riches
The Only Three Questions That Count
100 Minds That Made the Market
The Wall Street Waltz
Super Stocks

Fisher Investments Series
Own the World by Aaron Anderson
20/20 Money by Michael Hanson

Fisher Investments On Series
Fisher Investments on Energy
Fisher Investments on Materials
Fisher Investments on Consumer Staples
Fisher Investments on Industrials
Fisher Investments on Emerging Markets

FISHER
INVESTMENTS
PRESS

Fisher Investments on Emerging Markets

Fisher Investments

with

Austin B. Fraser

WILEY

John Wiley & Sons, Inc.

Published by John Wiley & Sons, Inc., Hoboken, New Jersey.

Published simultaneously in Canada.

For general information on our other products and services or for technical support, please contact our Customer Care Department within the United States at (800) 762-2974, outside the United States at (317) 572-3993 or fax (317) 572-4002.

Wiley also publishes its books in a variety of electronic formats. Some content that appears in print may not be available in electronic books. For more information about Wiley products, visit our web site at www.wiley.com.

Library of Congress Cataloging-in-Publication Data:

Fisher Investments on emerging markets / Fisher Investments, with Austin B. Fraser.
    p.   cm.
Includes bibliographical references and index.
ISBN 978-0-470-45236-3 (cloth)
    1. Investment analysis.   2. Investments, Foreign.   3. Securities.   4. Portfolio management.   I. Fraser, Austin B.   II. Fisher Investments.
HG4529.F58 2010
332.67'3—dc22   2009031921

Printed in the United States of America

10 9 8 7 6 5 4 3 2 1

Contents

Foreword

In your hands is the latest in a series of investing guides from Fisher Investments Press—the first ever imprint from a money manager, produced in partnership with John Wiley & Sons. But this guide is a bit different. Whereas the others have focused on analyzing standard investing sectors (Energy, Materials, Consumer Staples, Health Care, Industrials, etc.), this is the first guide on a region.

Why start with emerging markets? After all, the developed world seems risky enough without adding unique emerging market risks—political instability, poor infrastructure, corruption, and obscure regulations. Except that's not really true anymore. Once economic backwaters, emerging markets are increasingly civilized, orderly, booming nations—though individually, risks remain. Over the last 15 years, they've annualized 4.5 percent, accelerating to 5.8 percent in the last five years, while the developed world averaged just 3.0 percent. And, with that growth, their relative importance has grown, too—from 16 percent of total GDP in 1989 to 28 percent in 2009. And their stock markets have boomed—20 years ago they were just 1.4 percent of the world, 10 years ago 4.6 percent. Today, they're 12 percent and growing. You can't get good global exposure without owning some emerging markets now. Ignoring emerging markets means giving up opportunities to enhance performance and manage risk.

But don't be fooled—growth doesn't automatically mean good stock returns. Example: China's economy grew 10.1 percent in 2004 while its stocks fell 15.4 percent. So, with emerging markets booming, how can you know where to invest, and when? That's what this book shows. It teaches how to apply a top-down methodology to emerging markets that guides you in making the big decisions first. Simply: Making better big decisions—what asset class to hold, in what country or region, and in which sectors—will have bigger impact on longer term performance than individual stock picking. Though stock picking is and will always be important. This book can show you how.

For global investors, adding an emerging markets allocation is not only a logical progression but today a virtual imperative. Many emerging markets have immense natural resources and populations evolving toward middle class—vast untapped consumers as well as new human capital. And emerging market transparency continues to improve. Of course, many emerging markets still face political tumult, adding additional risk for stock picking in these nations. Some may emerge—like Israel, categorized as developed in 2009. Others, saddled by despotic governments and weak property rights, may submerge. But, as an overall category, you don't want to ignore nearly a third of the world—that's a sizable risk.

One thing this book won't give—and none of these guides provide—is hot stock tips for this year or any other. No book can give you stock tips worth following—claims otherwise are fairy tales. Instead, this book is intended to teach you a workable, repeatable framework for increasing the likelihood of finding profitable opportunities in emerging markets. This methodology should serve you not only this year or next, but the whole of your investing career, no matter what region or sector you analyze. So good luck and enjoy your tour of the emerging world.

Ken Fisher
CEO of Fisher Investments
Author of the *New York Times* best sellers
The Only Three Questions That Count,
The Ten Roads to Riches, and
How To Smell a Rat

Preface

The *Fisher Investments On* series is designed to provide individual investors, students, and aspiring investment professionals the tools necessary to understand and analyze investment opportunities, primarily for investing in global stocks.

Within the framework of a *top-down* investment (discussed more in Chapter 5), each guide is an easily accessible primer to economic sectors, regions, or other components of the global stock market. While this guide is specifically on emerging markets, the basic investment methodology is applicable for analyzing any region or even global sector, regardless of the current macroeconomic environment.

Why a top-down method? Vast evidence shows high-level, or *macro*, investment decisions are ultimately more important portfolio performance drivers than individual stocks. In other words, before picking stocks, investors can benefit greatly by first deciding if stocks are the best investment relative to other assets (like bonds or cash), and then choosing categories of stocks most likely to perform best on a forward-looking basis.

For example, a Technology sector stock picker in 1998 and 1999 probably saw his picks soar as investors cheered the so-called "New Economy." However, from 2000 to 2002, he probably lost his shirt. Was he just smarter in 1998 and 1999? Did his analysis turn bad somehow? Unlikely. What mattered most was stocks in general (and especially US technology stocks) did great in the late 1990s and poorly entering the new century. In other words, a top-down perspective on the broader economy was key to navigating markets—stock picking just wasn't as important.

Fisher Investments on Emerging Markets can help guide you in making top-down investment decisions specifically for emerging markets. It shows how to determine optimal times to invest more heavily in the region, how geo-political events have shaped the investing landscape and what to watch for in the future, and how individual stocks can benefit in various environments. Though frequently lumped together, each emerging market nation has its own local drivers, opportunities, and risks. Using our framework, you should be better equipped to critically analyze the region, spot opportunities, and avoid major pitfalls.

USING YOUR EMERGING MARKETS GUIDE

This guide is arranged into two sections. Part 1, "Going Backward to Move Forward," starts with a discussion of exactly what an emerging market is—because definitions vary, and how you approach the region can impact how you build an emerging market allocation. But its primary focus is a brief history of several key emerging market countries. Whereas developed markets, the US in particular, have long-standing, well-developed free markets, the road to a market economy in emerging regions is still being developed and often filled with potholes. An understanding of how they got to their current market constructs is vital in understanding where they're likely to go next—and how to game that for potentially superior returns.

Part 2, "Developing an Emerging Markets Strategy," delves into a top-down investment methodology, macro-economic and regional portfolio drivers, and individual security analysis—everything you need to know to build an emerging markets portfolio allocation. You'll learn to ask important questions like: What are the most important elements to consider when analyzing emerging markets—together and individually? What makes an emerging market stock different from its developed world peer? What are the greatest risks and red flags? This book gives you a step-by-step process to help differentiate countries and stocks so you can identify those with the greatest probability of outperforming. We'll also discuss a few investment strategies to help determine when and how to overweight specific nations or even sectors within the region.

Note: We've specifically kept the strategies presented here at a high level so you can return to the book for guidance no matter the market conditions. But we also can't possibly address every market scenario and how markets may change over time. And many additional considerations should be taken into account when crafting a portfolio strategy, including your own investment goals, your time horizon, and other factors unique to you. Therefore, you shouldn't rely solely on the strategies and pointers addressed here, because they won't always apply. Rather, this book is intended to provide general guidance and help you to begin thinking critically not only about emerging markets, but also investing in general.

Further, *Fisher Investments on Emerging Markets* won't give you a silver bullet for always picking the best stocks. The fact is, the right emerging markets stocks will be different in different climates and situations. Instead, this guide provides a framework for understanding the region so you can be dynamic and find information the market hasn't yet priced in. There won't be any stock recommendations, target prices, or even a suggestion whether now is a good time to be invested in a particular region. The goal is to provide you with tools to make these decisions for yourself, now and in the future. Ultimately, our aim is to give you the framework for repeated, successful investing. Enjoy.

Acknowledgments

Rarely is a book the product of one or two people, and this one is no exception. This project would have been impossible without the support and help of many colleagues and business relationships.

It is often said the job makes the man. Fortunately, I have had the pleasure of working with some of the brightest minds in finance. Both this project and my career are better for it. To begin, special thanks go to Ken Fisher, Andrew Teufel, Jeff Silk—the members of Fisher Investments' Investment Policy Committee. Without their dedication to building Fisher Investments into the world-class firm it is today, this opportunity would never have arisen. I am particularly grateful for their many years of tutelage as a member of their research staff.

I am also particularly grateful to Michael Hanson and Lara Hoffmans, not only for their patient mentoring and editing of this book—they were integral in turning this from a jumbled set of ideas into focused, well-polished prose—but for their substantial contribution to my lifelong pursuit of knowledge and intellectual betterment.

Several members of the Fisher Investments research staff also deserve thanks: Aaron Azelton, Theodore Gilliland, Dan Sinton, Brad Pyles, Erik Renaud, Brendan Erne, and Brian Kepp each provided key feedback and input throughout the process. And special thanks go to Matthew Schrader for breaking the bank and racking up pennies in library fines in the name of sound research.

Dina Ezzat deserves praise for adroitly managing logistics, from proper citations to its on-time delivery. Evelyn Chea helped put the finishing touches on the book by offering her copyediting expertise, and Leila Amiri offered valuable graphic design contributions, including the cover design.

Of course this book would also not be possible without our data vendors, and we owe a large debt of gratitude to Thomson Datastream, Thomson Reuters, MSCI, Inc., and Global Financial Data in particular for their permissions. I'd also like to extend appreciation to Fisher Investments' team at Wiley, for their support and guidance throughout this project, especially David Pugh and Kelly O'Connor.

Last, I would like to thank Carolyn Feng for her patience, understanding, and invaluable feedback during this challenging process—the book is substantially better because of her. And to my mother, Nancy: We will continue to live the lighter side.

GOING BACKWARD
TO MOVE FORWARD

1

THE FIVE Ws OF EMERGING MARKETS

Comprising 24 countries, 35 percent of the world's landmass, a whopping two-thirds of the world's nearly seven billion people, and almost a third of global output, emerging markets are fertile ground for the global investor.[1] These distant lands offer some of the most dynamic and unique opportunities—as investments, end markets for corporations seeking growth, or key cogs in the production of the world's goods. These prospects make emerging markets among the fastest growing segments of today's investing world.

Yet for all their allure, many avoid emerging markets out of fear, ignorance, or a belief they are radically different from developed world markets. This book aims to help shed light on these vital regions. To be clear, it won't tell you *where* to invest. Markets are too dynamic for that. By the time your eyes hit these pages, the market environment will have changed many times over. But we can demystify and take the fear out of investing in far-flung corners of the world, teaching you how to analyze this segment of the investing landscape for yourself.

To do so, you don't need a passport and a stack of plane tickets. See it this way: Many journalists don't write stories about events they've witnessed firsthand. More often than not, reporters uncover the details from others—experts or those who experienced something directly.[2] Using a variety of viewpoints, data, and internal perspectives developed over the years, we can do the same. To begin, we borrow an old-fashioned journalism technique—the five Ws—to lay the framework for the rest of this book.

WHO OR WHAT?

Who or what is an emerging market? This isn't a trick question. Any basic Internet search will get you more results than you could possibly peruse. This should provide more than enough information, right? Not quite. A single correct definition is far more important than many wrong ones. According to some of the results we found, an emerging market is:

> A foreign economy that is developing in response to the spread of capitalism and has created its own stock market.
>
> —*Answers.com*

> A financial market of a developing country, usually a small market with a short operating history.
>
> —*Investorwords.com*

> A euphemism for the world's poor countries, also known, often optimistically, as emerging economies.
>
> —*Economist.com*

It's evident there are a smattering of qualifiers—foreign, capitalism, poor, small, etc.; no doubt we could find dozens more in the Internet abyss. Yet what, for instance, does *small* mean? Is Indonesia, the fourth most populated country in the world, small? What about China, the third-largest economy?[3] Clearly, there are gray areas and plenty of conflicts. And where, for example, might the Investorwords. com definition lead you? Maybe you start looking for a market with a short operating history, thinking you'll be among the first to capitalize on the amazing growth potential therein. Hello, Zimbabwe! Bye-bye, retirement savings.

Truth is, there's no single definition of emerging markets that works as a sufficient catchall. America was an emerging market in the early 1800s. Same with Japan in the early 1960s. Even today, a poll of seasoned investment pros would certainly generate just as many answers. Fortunately, to successfully invest in emerging markets, you don't need to pin down an exact definition as much as understand the key characteristics they represent.

The following characteristics are not requirements to be part of emerging markets per se, but are generally found, to varying degrees, in most of them:

Fast-growing economies. In order to meet the demands of rapidly growing populations and shifts from agriculture to industry and production, emerging market economies are generally fast growing. A corollary is that emerging markets are characterized by a *rapid pace of change.* Many are familiar with China's economic growth story of the last decade, but Table 1.1 illustrates it has plenty of company.

Low levels of per capita income. On a per capita basis, emerging market countries are among the poorest. For example, Mexico's per capita income is $8,340 and Indonesia's is $1,650. By contrast, America's is $46,040.[5]

Relatively immature capital markets infrastructure. Emerging markets generally have poor reporting standards, a dearth of publicly available information, lack depth, and may be illiquid. They may also have weak regulatory frameworks.

Weak property rights. Private property rights are essential to a functioning marketplace, but such rights are usually not as ingrained in emerging markets. Investor capital may be unexpectedly taken away without due recourse.

Tenuous adherence to capitalist principles. Emerging market countries often embrace capitalism warily, eschew it in times of turbulence, or practice mercantilism operating under the guise of capitalism. Many still operate under explicit or implicit forms of communism and socialism.

Table 1.1   Average Annual Economic Growth

Developed	5-Year	10-Year	15-Year	25-Year
US	2.5%	2.5%	3.0%	3.1%
Japan	1.7%	1.3%	1.2%	2.2%
Germany	1.7%	1.5%	1.6%	2.1%
UK	2.3%	2.6%	2.9%	2.7%
Developed Market Average	*2.8%*	*2.8%*	*3.0%*	*2.9%*
Emerging	5-Year	10-Year	15-Year	25-Year
China	10.8%	9.7%	9.9%	10.1%
Brazil	4.7%	3.3%	3.2%	3.1%
Russia	7.0%	6.8%	2.7%	n/a
India	8.7%	7.1%	6.9%	6.2%
Korea	4.2%	5.3%	5.0%	6.3%
Mexico	3.4%	3.0%	2.9%	2.7%
Turkey	6.0%	3.8%	3.8%	4.4%
Indonesia	5.7%	4.8%	4.1%	4.9%
Poland	5.3%	4.2%	4.8%	3.2%
Taiwan	4.2%	3.8%	4.6%	6.1%
Emerging Market Average	*5.8%*	*4.7%*	*4.5%*	*4.4%*

Source: International Monetary Fund World Economic Outlook Database April 2009, MSCI, Inc.[4] Select countries chosen for illustrative purposes. Averages are inclusive of all countries within the MSCI World Index and MSCI Emerging Markets Index.

Varying political models. Authoritarianism, populism, democracy, single-party state, and many more. There are almost as many political models in emerging markets as there are countries, which have profound impacts on their capital markets.

Relatively underdeveloped institutions. Legal, judicial, and regulatory institutions tend to be weaker and less established.

Restrictions on foreign investors. Emerging markets generally don't have a long history of foreign investment, and there may be restrictions. For example, domestic Chinese shares are largely restricted to domestic investors; foreign investors must purchase American Depositary Receipts (ADRs) or Hong Kong-listed shares.

Freedom of foreign exchange and fund repatriation. You probably wouldn't invest your money in an Italian oil refiner unless you could change your money from euros back into US dollars, right? Emerging markets foreign exchange is often not as liberalized as the developed world, and some restrictions or extra regulations may need to be navigated.

Inherently risky. They have substantially higher levels of political, economic, and social risk compared to their developed market counterparts.

Emerging markets are not developed markets. Sure, it seems obvious, but it's important to distinguish what emerging markets are *not*. Developed markets are more developed and adhere to higher standards of many of the characteristics listed here. For example, the US, Australia, and Japan are developed markets.

American Depositary Receipts

American Depositary Receipts, commonly abbreviated as ADRs, are shares issued by a US bank that directly represent a specified number of shares in a foreign stock and are traded on US exchanges. For example, "TM" is the ticker for Toyota Motor Corporation shares traded on the New York Stock Exchange. One share of TM represents two shares of the foreign ordinary shares traded in Japan. ADRs are a good way for US investors to gain exposure to foreign companies, as they help reduce administrative costs and lower barriers to investing on foreign stock exchanges. We'll cover ADRs in more detail later on.

WHERE?

So who makes the grade? Which countries are typically classified as emerging markets? We could conduct an in-depth analysis of every country using the previous criteria, but there's an easier way to figure it out. A number of equity index providers have their own unique methodology to answer this question. We'll let them do the heavy lifting.

With so many index providers, intuitively you'd think they'd represent dramatically different stock universes. As it turns out, most of the criteria they use are similar to those we just covered. Table 1.2

Table 1.2   Emerging Market Country Coverage by Index Provider

Country	S&P	FTSE	MSCI
Argentina	✓	✓	✓
Brazil	✓	✓	✓
Chile	✓	✓	✓
China	✓	✓	✓
Colombia		✓	✓
Czech Republic	✓	✓	✓
Egypt	✓	✓	✓
Hungary	✓	✓	✓
India	✓	✓	✓
Indonesia	✓	✓	✓
Israel	✓	✓	✓
Korea	✓	✓	✓
Malaysia	✓	✓	✓
Mexico	✓	✓	✓
Morocco	✓	✓	✓
Pakistan		✓	✓
Peru	✓	✓	✓
Philippines	✓	✓	✓
Poland	✓	✓	✓
Russia	✓	✓	✓
South Africa	✓	✓	✓
Taiwan	✓	✓	✓
Thailand	✓	✓	✓
Turkey	✓	✓	✓
Total Countries	**22**	**24**	**24**

Source: FTSE, MSCI, Inc.[6], Standard & Poor's. As of 12/31/2008. S&P is the IFCI or Investable index; FTSE combines the Advanced and Secondary Emerging Markets Index; and MSCI is the MSCI Emerging Market Index.

shows the country composition of three major emerging markets index providers—Standard & Poor's (S&P), FTSE, and Morgan Stanley Capital International (MSCI). Aside from Colombia and Pakistan's absence in the S&P index, they're *exactly* the same.

As we'll discuss further in Chapter 5, choosing a benchmark is vital to long-term investment success. We need a road map for our journey—a well-constructed index to guide us. Any of these indexes are suitable choices. So pick one! For the purposes of this book, we'll mostly use the MSCI Emerging Markets Index. But any appropriately constructed index would do.

WHEN?

While many emerging market societies and cultures rank among the earliest in recorded history, they're relative newcomers to the investment world. Standard & Poor's, then known as Standard Statistics, developed its first US stock market index in 1923.[7] Emerging markets are spring chickens by comparison, barely in their college years.

The Third World No Longer

In September 1981, Antoine van Agtmael faced a dilemma. Working for the International Finance Corporation (IFC), a division of the World Bank, he'd just pitched a room full of money managers at Salomon Brothers headquarters in New York City on a "Third World Equity Fund." Van Agtmael made a successful pitch; the room ate it up. But an especially prescient manager at JP Morgan made an insightful point, "This is a very interesting idea you've got there, young man, but you will never sell it using the name 'Third World Equity Fund'!"

Van Agtmael realized he had a point. "Third World" was chock full of negative images—backwater villages, starving children, cheap manufactured goods. It certainly wasn't the slogan of an ideal sales pitch. After the meeting, van Agtmael came up with a term that sounded more positive and invigorating: Emerging Markets. In his words, "'Third World' suggested stagnation; 'Emerging Markets' suggested progress, uplift, and dynamism."[8]

Emerging market stocks were still a long way away from widespread acceptance. At the time of van Agtmael's speech, investors weren't terribly interested in what the rest of the world had to offer. Foreign stock ownership in the US was abysmally low—only 1.2 percent of portfolio holdings consisted of foreign equities in 1981—a common cognitive error called *home bias*.[9] Home bias is the tendency of investors to favor stocks in their home countries. For example, a US investor owning mostly US stocks is exhibiting home bias toward the US. Same with a German investor who owns mostly German stocks. Essentially, it's a failure to diversify properly—that is, globally.

The Third World

Did you know the term "Third World" developed during the Cold War to represent countries or regions in Africa and Asia not aligned in either the non-Communist or Communist blocs? Over time, it began to take on a completely different meaning, generally referring to underdeveloped nations.

An enterprising group of institutional investors recognized the potential in emerging markets. The Capital Group, one of the world's largest investment management organizations, opened its first emerging market fund in 1986. Templeton Investments, another famous US fund company, launched one in 1987 (its portfolio manager, Mark Mobius, remains a well-respected investment voice on emerging markets today). These funds raised awareness of emerging markets, and the asset class became increasingly popular. Private portfolio flows into emerging markets surpassed $50 billion in market capitalization by the end of the decade.[10] Though tiny compared to the many trillions of dollars in total equity holdings, it was evident a seed had been planted.

Germination by Indexation

If the 1980s were the formative years for emerging markets, the early 1990s were its adolescence. There was enthusiasm in a small but growing segment of the investment world, but emerging markets were still struggling to find an identity.

Wall Street played a large hand in its transition into adulthood. Up to this point, there was no clear understanding of what defined an emerging market. The Street recognized this, and several firms set out to create their own definitions. The International Finance Corporation published the first emerging market index in 1993 (creatively entitled the IFC Emerging Markets Index). Other indexes soon followed.

The introduction of indexes provided emerging markets investors with a common framework. Now there were explicit criteria to define an emerging market. It also gave professional money managers a benchmark to offer new products against. Stellar performance didn't hurt, either. From 1990 through 1994, the asset class returned an average annual 20.9 percent.[11] Money poured in—over $200 billion in 1993 and 1994 combined, more than doubling the total level of private portfolio investment.[12] Emerging markets had arrived.

Toward the end of the 1990s, a series of crises reminded investors of the risk in these nascent corners of the investment world. Billions were lost in the Tequila Crisis of 1994, Asian Financial Crisis of 1997 to 1998, and the Russian Ruble Crisis of 1998. These events and their legacies will be discussed in greater detail in subsequent chapters.

BRICs Lay the Foundation for the Twenty-First Century

But these crises weren't enough to shake investor sentiment for long. Emerging markets were here to stay. After the upheaval, a period of stabilization and growth renewed confidence. In fact, many began to question whether some emerging markets were really even "emerging" anymore. In 2001, Goldman Sachs coined the acronym "BRIC" for "Brazil, Russia, India, and China." The investment bank believed these countries shouldn't be thought of as emerging markets in the classical sense—they were now critical and integral to an ever-growing globalized world. In a short 20 years, emerging markets had gone from an unknown to one of the most popular asset classes of the twenty-first century.

THE MOST IMPORTANT QUESTION—WHY?

Despite their ascendancy into the popular investment lexicon, conventional wisdom still views emerging markets as appropriate only for speculators or gamblers—those with abnormally high risk tolerance. These are assets meant for high-flying professionals or investors with a time horizon of 30 to 40 years, the wisdom says. For the rest of us, emerging markets should play little to no role in your portfolio. Why is this discouraging view so widespread?

The answer is rooted in fear. There's good sense behind this—emerging markets can be risky and uncertain, and investing in them, intimidating. Maybe you remember stories of entire countries nearly going bankrupt in the late 1990s. Or perhaps you're just put off by their *strangeness*. After all, their languages, business practices, political systems, freedoms of speech, and so on can be substantially different from the Western investing world. It's just plain easier to stick to what you know (and thus feel most comfortable with)—hence the tendency toward home bias.

But emerging markets *should* play a vital role in a properly constructed global portfolio of equities. Otherwise, you're forfeiting a huge opportunity. In today's global investment landscape, emerging markets make up an increasingly bigger piece of the pie. In 1988, emerging markets constituted a mere 1 percent of the MSCI All-Country World Index, MSCI's broadest index covering all developed and emerging market countries. By the end of 2007, this total had risen to a whopping 11.3 percent[13] (see Figure 1.1).

These aren't companies to ignore, either. In fact, they're some of the largest in the world. In 2001, there was only one company in emerging markets with a market capitalization greater than $50 billion out of 68 in the entire world. By the end of 2007, there were 21 (out of 170). Companies this size are well known globally. Heard of American Express

Figure 1.1   MSCI Emerging Index Market Value as a Percent of the MSCI All-Country World Index
Source: Thomson Datastream; MSCI Inc.[14]

($61 billion)? How about Kraft Foods ($51 billion)? We'd also be willing to bet you've heard of many emerging market companies too without even realizing it. Know anyone with a television made by Samsung? That's Samsung Electronics, an $87 billion South Korean technology company. No rational investor should restrict themselves from investing in some of the biggest and most dynamic companies in the world.[15]

BUT HOW?

"But wait!" you say. "You must have flunked journalism school! You've forgotten one more crucial question: the How!" Don't fret, that's what the remainder of this book entails.

To move forward, we must first move backward. Chapters 2 through 4 will illustrate, through historical narrative, the characteristics outlined here. Investing is about probabilities, not certainties. And history is the only rational way we can reasonably begin to assess probabilities for what might happen in the future. It enables us to see the interconnections, to make smarter investment decisions, and to realize what is truly unique about now, or what is being repeated.

Each of the next three chapters focuses on a different region of the MSCI Emerging Markets Index—Asia, Latin America, and Europe, the Middle East & Africa (EMEA)—through the historical lens of boom and bust. This may scare some readers. Volatility is always present in investing—especially in emerging markets. Certain countries and sectors outperform others at various points in time and sometimes by large margins. But correctly identifying these drivers is a critical variable to your success. With that in mind, the next several chapters are not intended to frighten you away from the category but instead to help you better understand its historical context and the differences across regions. In the long run, investing in emerging markets can be a good decision—the MSCI Emerging Markets Index returned an average annualized 11 percent in the 21 years ending in 2008.[16]

Armed with a historical perspective, we move on to discuss the tools required to successfully invest in emerging markets. Chapter 5 provides a layout of the emerging markets land today. We'll cover which countries and sectors hold the most influence and learn a distinct way of thinking about these markets that offers the best chance of investment success. Chapter 6 discusses developing portfolio drivers, a critical step in determining the areas of the market expected to perform differently than the whole. Only after you've developed portfolio drivers should you begin to think about picking stocks—a brief discussion of security selection comprises Chapter 7. Last, Chapter 8 provides a practical guide to the types of instruments and strategies an emerging market investor might use and common challenges faced.

2

LIONS, TIGERS, AND DRAGONS, *OH MY!*

Tigers are revered in East Asia as both religious and cultural icons. They are the national animal in some countries and appear on the flags of others. Dominant throughout consumer culture, their likeness peddles everything from airlines to candy. For all their symbolism of power and strength, however, wild tigers face oblivion. The March 28, 1994 issue of *Time* magazine was ominously entitled "Doomed. Why the Regal Tiger Is on the Brink of Extinction."

The financial history of East Asia has fascinating parallels with the history of its feline mascot. The latter part of the twentieth century was a time of explosive growth for economies in the region. The World Bank famously popularized this phenomenon with its seminal report in 1993 entitled "The East Asian Miracle."[1] But, much like the fate of the wild tiger, the region teetered on the edge of collapse by the end of the decade as the Asian Financial Crisis decimated economies and markets. A thorough analysis of this period will leave investors with a fundamental understanding of its legacies and how it shapes policies and market behavior to this day.

Finally, no view of Asia would be complete without a discussion of the 800-pound dragon in the room, China. Largely unscathed by the aforementioned financial crisis, it went from Communist afterthought to one of the world's most powerful and intimidating economic forces in mere decades. Yet, despite its economic prowess, its relevance to markets is often misunderstood. An understanding of China's recent capital markets history is equally crucial to investment success in the region.

ROAR OF THE TIGERS

Our story begins with a roar. In the 30 years from 1965 to 1994, the 23 economies comprising East Asia grew faster collectively than any other region in the world. Growth was strongest in Hong Kong, South Korea, Singapore, and Taiwan (known as the "Four Tigers"), and in the newly industrialized Southeast Asian nations of Indonesia, Malaysia, and Thailand.[2] In the 1980s, Japan's economic rise captured the attention of economists and investors. Many saw a similar phenomenon in these small neighboring nations, and stellar economic growth rates—7.5 percent annually during the 30-year period—seemed to confirm this optimism. Talk of the world's economic center of gravity shifting eastwards was commonplace.

Not surprisingly, Asian stock markets soared. While historical data are limited, in the six years ending 1993, MSCI Emerging Asia equities returned an average annualized 30 percent. (See Table 2.1.) In 1993 alone, they returned a whopping 100 percent in US dollars![3] The "Asian Miracle" was born.

Yet, miracles manifest in the eye of the beholder. A lifelong Chicago Cubs fan might see divine intervention at work should its perennially cursed baseball team finally win the World Series. But in an economic sense, miracles are bound by the natural laws governing markets. The "Asian Miracle" was no different. It may have seemed like a miracle at the time, but the region's remarkable economic record was instead rooted in a series of positive fundamental developments.

Table 2.1   MSCI Emerging Asia Stock
Market Returns

1989	68.8%	1999	69.4%
1990	−17.5%	2000	−41.8%
1991	9.9%	2001	6.2%
1992	18.9%	2002	−4.7%
1993	99.8%	2003	51.0%
1994	−14.4%	2004	15.3%
1995	−5.7%	2005	27.5%
1996	2.9%	2006	33.2%
1997	−48.2%	2007	41.6%
1998	−11.0%		

Source: Thomson Datastream, MSCI Inc.[4]

Macroeconomic Stability

In contrast with other developing nations where boom-and-bust cycles led to wild fluctuations in economic activity, Asian countries were largely successful in fostering macroeconomic stability. This stability, rooted in sound economic and public policy, was a key driver behind the boom.

A major component was fiscal prudence. The level of deficits was not markedly better in Asia than other emerging market regions, but governments were largely more responsible with public funds. Many introduced measures to rein in spending, such as Indonesia's balanced budget law or Thailand's exchange rate management framework, which resembled a gold standard. In addition, spending was easily financed by fast economic growth, high savings rates, and low debt levels. Thus, the region avoided inflationary excess money creation that destabilized other areas like Latin America.[5]

Inflation in Asia was not particularly low by developed market standards at the time—in some countries it surpassed double digits (as is often the case in developing regions). But it compared favorably to other high-growth emerging markets. For example, in the 10 years from 1984 to 1995, the average annual inflation rate in emerging Asia was 7 percent. The same measure for emerging Europe, the Middle East, & Africa (a common regional grouping) was 49 percent.[6] Even more critical was its consistency—the huge inflationary spikes of decades past disappeared. Steady and lower inflation kept real interest rates stable and the cost of capital predictable, a critical driver propelling investment and business activity.

While exchange rate policy shifted periodically throughout the boom, it too was prudently managed. Unlike Latin American countries, Asian nations rarely used currency as a tool to fight inflation (arguably because it was never necessary). Big swings in the real exchange rate were uncommon.

Last, governments were quick to respond with policy adjustments in times of stress. For example, as an oil importer, Indonesia faced rapidly worsening terms of trade caused by declining oil prices. The government responded decisively and devalued the rupiah in 1983 and 1986, cut expenditures, and rescheduled costly capital-intensive projects. The quick response reined in the country's deficit, staving off a much larger shock.[7]

High Savings and Investment

High savings and investment rates were also byproducts of macroeconomic stability and rapid economic growth during Asia's economic boom. Many suggest culture plays a role in how much a society saves, noting that Asians traditionally put away more than any other group in the world. While these factors may have had some bearing on behavior in Asia, the government played a key role, too. It instituted many policies—some good, some bad—to ensure the economic bounty was saved and invested.

First, the good:

- **Property rights were relatively well protected.** Property rights are crucial to well-functioning capital markets and economies. If property rights are not secure, there is little incentive to invest. Developing regions usually lag developed nations in this respect, and incremental improvements can make a big difference.
- **Sound tax policy.** Low effective tax rates meant the populace kept more of their money, encouraging private savings and

investment. Governments achieved this through a variety of measures. Taiwan, for example, had very low levels of effective income taxes due to extensive exemptions. Meanwhile, Hong Kong more directly maintained low marginal rates—around 15 percent for personal taxes and 17.5 percent for businesses.

- **Postal savings institutions.** So called because they were located in government post offices, these were essentially financial institutions backed by the government. They offered small savers greater security and lower transaction costs than the private sector and were thus successful in attracting poorer and rural households. Until these systems were developed, rural citizens were often shut out of the financial system. While such policy involved the government, it proved worthwhile because it promoted saving at the rural level.

But there was also bad:

- **"Forced saving" programs.** Many governments instituted a variety of "forced saving," like mandatory pension schemes, restrictions on consumption and limitations on borrowing for consumption (e.g., purchases on credit). For example, Malaysia and Singapore had mandatory pension plans for their citizens. While an effective policy in the short term (people usually do what you tell them when forced), it had negative implications for the long term as it restricted the free flow of capital.
- **Restricted capital flows.** Savings and investments abroad were often disallowed. The logic here is straightforward: If investors can't send money out of the country, they'll invest domestically instead. Japan, Korea, and Taiwan all did this. But it's bad for investors because it ultimately restricts the investment universe and leads to pricing dislocations.
- **Artificially low interest rates.** Governments intervened to hold interest rates below market levels to encourage investment. This caused distortions and imbalances as holding interest rates low for too long creates a disincentive to save, but high rates can restrict investment.

Whatever the individual merits of each policy, they generally worked as a whole to stimulate savings and investment. Consider the case of Singapore, where investment as a percentage of output rose from 11 percent to more than 40 percent between 1966 and 1990—a massive investment in physical capital.[8] Virtually every country in the region went through a similar adjustment.

Export-Driven Growth

Emerging market countries generally don't have a sufficient middle class to demand goods as a source of internal growth like the developed world. Governments realized manufacturing and exporting provided an alternative and in the 1960s and 1970s underwent a period of massive industrialization, adopting export-driven growth models. Today, a disproportionate amount of clothes, shoes, and home electronics—a huge portion of our consumable goods—are manufactured in Asia and shipped to households or storefronts around the world. The approach varied across countries, but each government generally pursued export-friendly policies. The ensuing export push further fueled the economic boom.

To encourage exports, many countries sought to avoid an appreciating local currency, and in some cases purposely undervalued theirs. A strong currency makes a country's exports more expensive (and its imports less costly) and thus less competitive. To see why, imagine you're a manager at Don's Dishwashers, a dishwasher manufacturer located in Taiwan. You sell most of your goods to Ken's Kitchen Wholesalers in the US. The current exchange rate between Taiwan and the US is two to one, which means your 200 Taiwanese dollar dishwasher costs Ken 100 US dollars. Now imagine that the exchange rate depreciates, and it now takes three Taiwanese dollars to buy one US dollar. What does your dishwasher cost Ken now? 33 percent less, or $66.67! That's incentive for Ken to buy more goods from Don—a happy situation for both!

But how did governments accomplish this? Most countries in the region maintained a *fixed exchange rate*, meaning their currency was pegged to the US dollar. When a country pegs its currency to another, the exchange rate between the two barely moves. This process doesn't happen naturally—a country maintaining a pegged currency will be forced to buy or sell its currency to keep its value close to the pegged value. For example, Hong Kong maintains a US dollar peg, currently at 7.75 Hong Kong dollars to one US dollar.[9] Imagine that the demand for Hong Kong condominiums is exceptionally strong. Real estate speculators rush to trade in their foreign currency for Hong Kong dollars to get in on the action, pushing its value up—the more something is demanded, the higher its price. But since the Hong Kong government maintains a peg, it is forced to *sell* Hong Kong dollars into the currency market to counteract the upward pressure from the real estate speculators.

Exchange rates were manipulated in other ways to favor exporters. Some, like South Korea, used different effective exchange rates for exports and imports through subsidies, tax breaks, and tariffs. Others, like Indonesia, simply adjusted the exchange rate through large devaluations.

Governments also practiced protectionism in the form of subsidies and tariffs. For example, they granted domestic exporters duty-free imports on the capital and intermediate goods necessary to manufacture their exports while continuing to protect domestic consumer goods from foreign competition.

Devaluation

Devaluation is a substantial drop in the value of a currency. There is no formal threshold distinguishing mere depreciation from devaluation. Every currency is different—a 30 percent drop in the Brazilian real may not be that large given its history of steep gains and declines, but a similar fall in the Malaysian ringgit would be huge since it's generally less volatile. Generally, devaluations aren't market-created—the government usually intervenes and intentionally causes the drop in currency.

Governments may devalue their currency for many reasons. Often, it's done for economic motives, such as improving export competitiveness. Other times, it may be cruel necessity. For example, if a country is a net debtor (runs a current account deficit) and finds itself unable to meet its foreign obligations, it may be forced to devalue. The devaluation means it would owe less money to its creditors (since its currency is worth less), assuming it was able to borrow in its own currency.

Financial Liberalization

Later in the economic reform process, governments turned their attention to liberalizing the financial sector, which helped the boom continue. Interest rates were deregulated, competition stimulated, and regulatory systems reformed. Many financial markets and exchanges we know today were born during this time.

TO THE BRINK OF EXTINCTION—THE ASIAN FINANCIAL CRISIS

If you stopped reading here, you'd leave with the impression Asia was a one-way ticket to prosperity. Near the end of the century, everything appeared to confirm this thinking. Investors were convinced the region's extraordinary economic growth record meant it was immune to traditional business cycles (i.e., "it's different this time").

But, of course, nothing is ever different this time. No investment segment stays on top forever, and the East Asian boom was no different. A crisis of unforeseen proportions ripped through the region in 1997 to 1998, leaving not just companies but entire *countries* on the brink of collapse. Ironically, many of the characteristics fostering the economic miracle in the first half of the decade left the region needing just that to survive.

A Brief Timeline: A Baht Out of Hell

The exact cause of the Asian Financial Crisis is open to debate (we'll discuss that in a moment), but the trigger point is widely accepted—a run on Thailand's currency, the baht. By the mid-1990s, some of the luster of the Asian economic boom began to wear off. The devaluations of the Chinese yuan and Japanese yen along with a sharp decline in semiconductor prices weighed on export revenues and overall economic activity. In Thailand, these events were accompanied by speculative pressures on the baht.[10]

Beginning in May 1997, Thailand began to spend billions of dollars of its foreign currency reserves defending its currency from speculative attacks. Then, on July 2, 1997, after months of saying it would do nothing of the sort, Thailand abandoned its efforts to maintain its peg to the US dollar. Its currency plummeted as much as 20 percent, reaching all-time lows.

Foreign Exchange Reserves

Foreign exchange reserves, or currency reserves, are foreign currency deposits held by a country's central bank. Almost all countries hold currency reserves, but their motives for doing so differ widely. Some reasons include:

- Exchange rate policy—for fixed currency regimes, reserves allow officials to adjust for normal changes in supply and demand. In other cases, it can be used to achieve a specific economic aim, like maintaining a weak currency to aid exporters.
- Limiting external vulnerability by maintaining foreign currency liquidity to absorb shocks when access to borrowing is limited.
- Servicing foreign currency liabilities and debts.
- Providing a level of confidence to international markets by assuring a country can meet its international obligations.
- As a defense against national disasters or emergencies.

Foreign currency reserves are primarily accumulated in four ways:

1. Borrowing foreign currency formally through an international bond offering.
2. Borrowing foreign currency against domestic currency in the foreign currency swap market.
3. Buying it outright against domestic currency.
4. Gathering it via current account surpluses, where exporters exchange foreign currency with the central bank.

Thailand's devaluation rippled through the Asian region with alarming speed, first affecting nations deemed vulnerable to similar financial and economic problems. Within just a few days, the Malaysian central bank intervened to defend its currency, the ringgit. The Philippine peso devalued on July 11. Indonesia also floated its currency, the rupiah, on August 14. Figure 2.1 demonstrates the severity of the region's currency sell-off. By the time the crisis reached South Korea, the then 11th

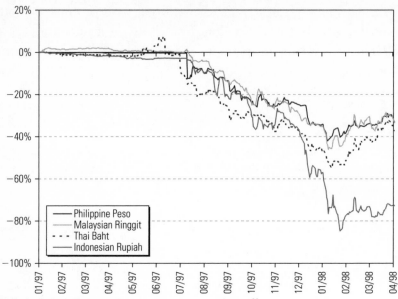

Figure 2.1   Asian Currencies vs. US Dollar
Source: Thomson Datastream.

largest economy in the world, worries of a global financial meltdown were pervasive.

Big devaluations soon gave way to worries of financial stability, as deteriorating bank balance sheets led to widespread bankruptcies. Devaluations are a double whammy to firms—they make assets worth less and liabilities increase. In an attempt to restore order and confidence, Asian nations began calling on the help of international aid organizations. On August 5, Thailand adopted tough economic measures proposed by the IMF in return for a loan of $17 billion. Thailand's government shuttered 42 financial firms as part of the IMF's austerity measures (another 56 were closed in December). In October 1997, Indonesia received an IMF loan package of $40 billion and closed 16 insolvent banks (by the end of the crisis, it would have entered into four separate agreements with the IMF). And in December, South Korea got the biggest of them all—$57 billion.[11]

The crisis soon began to test the social and political order. For example, in early January, Indonesians fearing economic collapse began to clear store shelves of food and staple items. Prices for basic food staples leapt 80 percent a week later. By May, demonstrations protesting these steep increases denounced President Suharto's administration. When troops fired on a peaceful protest at a Jakarta university, killing six and sparking week-long riots, Suharto's 32-year reign as Indonesian president was doomed.

Next, things spilled over to rest of the world in a phenomenon called *contagion*. The Dow Jones Industrial Average fell 554 points on October 27, 1997, the biggest daily point loss ever to that point, as the broader turmoil weighed on confidence in the US. One of Japan's largest brokerage firms went bankrupt in early November. Others soon followed. And many other countries, such as Brazil and Russia, saw similar sell-offs. (The crisis set off a separate, concurrent crisis in Russia that will be explored in Chapter 4.)[12]

Contagion

Contagion is a common investment term used to describe the transmission of a crisis across many countries, including those not fundamentally linked to its cause. The Asian Financial Crisis is often referred to as contagion because equities across the world suffered, not just Asia's. The World Bank website (www.worldbank.org) has a useful discussion on the topic, with more definitions and links to in-depth research.

By the end of 1998, the carnage was unmistakable. MSCI Emerging Asia equities *fell* 48 percent in 1997, compared to a 16 percent *rise* in the MSCI World.[13] But even that vicious decline masks the true damage, as the index was buoyed by countries like Taiwan and India that were relatively unaffected by the crisis. Many of the countries hardest hit lost more than two-thirds of their value. Economic growth also ground to halt—a miracle no longer. Table 2.2 shows each country's stock market in 1997 and economic performance the following year.

Table 2.2   The Aftermath: Equity Markets & Economic Growth Plummet

Country	1997 MSCI Market Return	1998 GDP Growth
China	−25.3%	7.8%
India	11.3%	6.0%
Indonesia	−74.1%	−13.1%
Korea	−66.7%	−6.9%
Malaysia	−68.0%	−7.4%
Pakistan	28.1%	2.6%
Philippines	−62.6%	−0.6%
Taiwan	−6.3%	4.5%
Thailand	−73.4%	−10.5%
Emerging Markets	**−11.6%**	**1.1%**
Emerging Asia	**−48.2%**	**0.8%**

Source: Thomson Datastream; MSCI, Inc,[14] International Monetary Fund. Emerging Markets and Emerging Asia GDP figures represent nominal GDP-weighted real growth.

CRISIS CAUSES

The devastation of the crisis is clear. Less so is the cause. Three major theories have emerged: a classic mania and panic, an inevitable crisis triggered by the run on the Thai baht, or austerity measures by the IMF exacerbating what would have otherwise been a bump in the road. It was probably some combination of the three, with an emphasis on many of the economic and industrial policies that led to the boom in previous decades. Each, however, leaves us with important legacies for investing in the region today.

Mania Brought Down by Panic

Manias and panics are recurring phenomena in financial markets.[15] While the cause of each is distinct, they have a common theme: Enthusiasm for a market or asset rapidly loses touch with reality. Asset prices rise to extraordinary heights before confidence and greed turn to fear and despair, sending markets into a tailspin.

In 1637, tulip mania hit the Netherlands. Prices of the newly introduced flower reached more than 20 times the annual income of a skilled craftsman.[16] In 1711, the South Sea Company attracted a flood of investment after buying the rights to *all* trade in the South Seas for a £10 million IOU. Poor management failed to deter interest in the stock, which reached £1,000 (unadjusted for inflation) before plummeting to zero when the South Sea Bubble burst.[17] More recently, technology mania in the late 1990s spurred a proliferation of technology company IPOs, though many had operations that were not fundamentally viable. Equities of companies with no real earnings reached stratospheric heights before collapsing in 2000.

The Asian economic "miracle" showed many of the same characteristics. Stock returns, as previously mentioned, inflated fast—doubling in 1993 alone. Other asset classes (like real estate) also witnessed explosive demand growth. For example, from 1990 to 1997, nearly one million new housing units were registered in Thailand. That was more than double the previous two decades combined.[18]

Similarities also existed on the way down. Panic set in when investors realized Asia wasn't the investing panacea they thought it was. The sharp reversal in Thailand's capital account is evidence of investors running for the exits. As shown in Figure 2.2, the country's

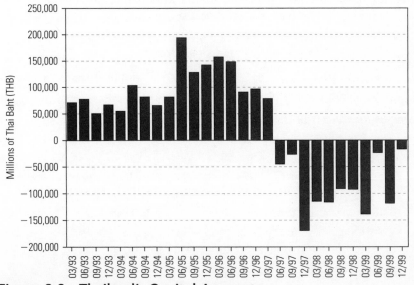

Figure 2.2   Thailand's Capital Account

Source: Thomson Datastream.

capital account averaged around 100 billion baht through 1995 and 1996, illustrating a net inflow of foreign capital. By 1997, however, it plunged to a deficit greater than 150 billion baht. A similar fate occurred in other Asian countries.

But manias and panics are behavioral in nature and therefore difficult to prove. Asia in the late 1990s did exhibit many of the symptoms of classic manias, and the panic exodus of capital certainly

---

Balance of Payments 101

Balance of payments data are usually broken into two distinct categories—the current account and the capital account. The two exactly offset each other by definition—that is, if a country runs a current account deficit, it runs an equal-sized capital account surplus.

The current account is pretty straightforward. The vast majority of it is the trade balance (exports minus imports). It also includes some funny add-ons like income from investment and unilateral transfers like international aid. But those are generally tiny and can be ignored for the most part. As an example, let's analyze what would cause Mexico's current account to increase. (Note that the exact opposite leads to a decrease.)

- A **depreciation of the peso** makes Mexican exports more competitive, increasing the trade balance and thus the current account.
- A **slowing Mexican economy** would decrease imports as people would generally buy less. This would also cause the trade balance and current account to increase.
- An **increase in growth in other foreign economies** would increase demand for Mexican exports, thus increasing the current account.

The capital account records all transactions involving change in the ownership of an asset. This investment is usually broken down into three categories:

1. **Foreign direct investment**, or FDI, is foreign ownership of domestic assets. It often refers to tangible assets (e.g., a US firm spending $100 million to build a factory in Mexico).
2. **Portfolio investment** measures the amount of money flowing into an economy through the purchase of securities, such as equities and bonds.
3. **Other investment** consists of changes in the holdings of loans, bank accounts, and currencies.

An increase in the capital account occurs when more capital flows in than out, either through tangible assets or other investment.

exacerbated an already dire situation. But a spate of fundamental economic imbalances suggests there was much more at work.

An Inevitable Financial Crisis

Another school of thought argues rapid economic growth disguised fundamental weaknesses that existed for decades in the Asian financial system. This argument regards the run on the Thai baht as merely a tipping point to an inevitable crisis. There are some truths to this story, rooted in two factors.

International Borrowing   A crucial part of Asia's economic ascendancy was access to foreign capital. As mentioned in Chapter 1, emerging markets are riskier, thus commanding higher risk premiums. In other words, investors require at least the potential for greater reward in return for taking extra risk. As such, interest rates in emerging markets tend to be higher than the developed world. A 12 percent interest rate would appear like highway robbery to the average US homebuyer, but rates that high (and even higher) are commonplace in emerging markets. Asia in the late 1990s was no exception.

High interest rates had ramifications for the region's banks. Banks are in the *maturity transformation* game. They accept short-term deposits—liabilities—and use that money to issue long-term loans—assets. This is the basic way any bank does business and is extremely profitable if long-term interest rates (what they *receive*) are notably higher than short-term interest rates (what they *pay*).

Under this model, Asian financial institutions willingly offered loans at the prevailing higher interest rates. But they were understandably averse to paying out high interest rate deposits to fund those loans. Thus, in order for an Indonesian bank to make a loan in its local currency, for example, it was tempted to accept low-interest funding in other currencies instead of relatively high interest rupiah deposits. This happened across much of Asia at the time.

Such a model in itself isn't necessarily a bad thing. After all, emerging economies often need foreign capital to grow. But emerging markets are characterized by immature capital markets infrastructure. In Asia's case, this meant underdeveloped bond and derivative markets, leaving banks without the necessary tools to hedge currency exposure. Although most bank lending was denominated in domestic currencies, the liability side of the balance sheet was saddled with substantial amounts of unhedged currency risk. The tendency to take on this foreign currency risk was even greater because of their US dollar pegs. In normal times, this exposure didn't pose too much of a problem. But this period was far from normal.

Hedging

A *hedge* is an investment intended to mitigate the risk in another investment. Generally, investors hedge because they wish to minimize their exposure to an unwanted risk while still allowing the ability to profit from the investment. Today, virtually every company in the world does some form of hedging. For example, an airline may hedge the price of jet fuel so it knows it will never pay more than a certain price for its primary input cost. Or a bank borrowing money in a foreign currency may wish to mitigate the impact of foreign currency movements in the repayment of its loan.

When Asian nations broke their US dollar pegs and devalued, their high levels of debt held in foreign currency had disastrous consequences. Why is this so? Let's say you're an Indian bank and accept a $100 investment from an American banker and the current rupee exchange rate is 30 rupees per one US dollar. As of today, you owe 300 rupees to the banker. Now, let's say the exchange rate suddenly goes to 60 rupees to one US dollar, or a 50 percent devaluation (similar to moves in many of the countries involved in the Asian Financial Crisis). How many rupees do you owe now? Twice as many—600! In a matter of months, many Asian banks saw the size of their liabilities more than double. Even the healthiest bank would be hard-pressed to survive a shock like that. But Asian banks were especially vulnerable. Bank management, regulators, international investors, and government officials all underestimated the risk of such exposure.

Government-Directed Lending Another key driver behind the Asian economic boom was directed credit. At the time, government-directed lending was crucial to economic growth. Capital market infrastructure was lacking and the banking system poorly developed. Arguably, someone had to fill the void. But no government, emerging or developed market, allocates capital very well. Always and everywhere, private institutions and free markets do a better job. The unintended consequences of public involvement were evident in every country, but we'll focus on the chaebol structure in South Korea as it offers some of the most egregious examples.

Park Chung Hee, leader of the military coup that took control of South Korea in 1961, emphasized state control of the economy and the promotion of large corporations and conglomerates, or *chaebol.* Initially, these were firms that showed the most success in the export-driven push described earlier in this chapter. While subsequent governments tried to pry influence from the chaebols, many still exist today. For example, Samsung may be a familiar name as an electronics maker. But that's only one out of many companies in the family— Samsung Securities, Samsung Fire & Marine, Samsung Engineering & Construction, etc.

In order to control and support the chaebol system, Park allocated low-interest loans through state-controlled banks. This created an alliance between the government, large corporations, and the financial system that underpinned the economy. The government also gave these firms assurances that credit, tax exemptions, and other support would remain available. Within this vast interconnected web, corruption flourished. It was an arrangement that would make even Don Corleone proud.

With access to cheap capital implicitly backed by the government, the chaebol went on a feeding frenzy. By the early 1990s, the largest 30 chaebol accounted for 49 percent of assets and 42 percent of sales in the manufacturing sector.[19] This boom was fueled almost exclusively by debt: The debt-to-equity ratio of all Korean manufacturing firms was a whopping 3.96 in 1997. That is, for every Korean won of a firm's equity, there was nearly four won of debt behind it! To give you an idea of how extreme that is, the US manufacturing average was 1.54 at the time.[20]

Such high leverage left the financial system vulnerable to shock, and the Asian Financial Crisis was just that. Bankruptcies were rife as the financial system essentially collapsed. Daewoo Group was the most infamous default, with $80 billion in unpaid debt.[21] At the time, it was the largest bankruptcy in history—not just in emerging markets, but the world.

The chaebol and South Korea illustrate two inherent flaws with directed credit: Banks are not free to allocate capital based on economic interest and the implicit guarantee behind government-backed credit encourages risky behavior because losses are limited. Directed credit had built an economic juggernaut on a faulty foundation.

IMF Austerity

Other observers heaped blame on the IMF, arguing its actions precipitated the crisis. The IMF is tasked with the lofty aspiration of safeguarding the stability of the international monetary system, which was clearly shaken by the crisis. In a bid to restore confidence, the organization immediately offered assistance.

In 1997, the IMF arranged $35 billion in support for the three countries most affected by the crisis—Thailand, Indonesia, and South Korea. They also arranged an additional $77 billion in financing from multilateral and bilateral sources. By 1998, due to additional assistance needed by Indonesia, these figures increased another $1.3 billion and $5 billion, respectively—nearly $120 billion in total aid. The loan arrangements were to be used to meet foreign debt payments that the countries otherwise couldn't afford. It was an unprecedented intervention.[22]

In return for assistance, the IMF forced countries to adopt a series of austerity measures. This is where many believe the organization made matters worse. They imposed tough measures: monetary policy tightening, harsh fiscal austerity, and larger longer-term structural reforms. Many criticized these requirements as unnecessary or misdirected. For example, the IMF instructed the recipient nations to dramatically cut spending. But, as we saw earlier, Asian nations had huge amounts of savings, and governments were running budget surpluses. Cutting spending was arguably unnecessary (and possibly counterproductive), furthering recessionary pressures. Also, the required shuttering of banks, ostensibly done to strengthen the financial system, had the opposite effect as depositors began pulling money out of all banks, healthy or not.[23]

Interestingly, crisis-inflicted Malaysia was the only country that refused IMF assistance and advice. Despite some bumps on the road, it successfully navigated the crisis. Many take this as evidence the countries should have been left alone.

But for all the blame heaped on the IMF, it's often forgotten that the countries themselves were at fault as well. Political wavering was commonplace. Asian leaders were fiercely guarded and the loan packages unpopular. Governments took too long to draft up new economic plans and longer still to actually implement them. In South Korea, presidential candidates in the December 1997 elections loudly disavowed the program, raising questions whether agreed-upon aid would even find its way to the country.

In retrospect, the IMF perhaps didn't fully appreciate the crisis was different from past examples—the problem didn't lay with the handling of the economy by the government. Instead, it was mostly the private sector (albeit heavily aided and abetted by government policies). Fair or not, the organization received a large portion of the blame for making matters worse. To this day, it's viewed warily throughout Asia, and government policy in the aftermath has partly focused on never having to call on its help ever again. It's a bit too simplistic to say that everything would have worked out fine without the IMF, but it certainly contributed to the pain.

LESSONS AND LEGACIES

More than 10 years later, what relevance does the Asian Financial Crisis have for investors today? The answer is quite a lot. To be clear, none of the following provides answers on how to avoid the next crisis. Understanding the legacies of the crisis, however, gives investors important context.

Contagion

The Asian Financial Crisis taught the investing world the concept of *contagion*. The crisis originated in a small country but soon spread globally to much larger, more developed economies. Why was it so virulent? There is no single answer. Some say Thailand's collapse served as a wake-up call to investors to re-evaluate other emerging markets. When similar problems were discovered, the crisis spread. Others believe sheer panic was the cause—investors were so alarmed by the crisis they abruptly pulled their investments out of all assets viewed as risky. Whatever it was, the Asian Financial Crisis showed us that correlations between emerging market countries are highest during crises (i.e., their markets all decline).

The Vicious Cycle of Currency Crises

The Asian Financial Crisis was first and foremost a currency crisis. The dislocations in the region's currency markets exposed the underlying weakness of the financial system.

In many ways, currency crises are self-fulfilling. While some currency weakness helps export competitiveness, too much is bad—it breeds economic instability. Foreign investors run for the exits as the value of investments declines precipitously along with the currency. The currency comes under further attack from speculators looking to profit from further falls. This is a vicious cycle—a weak currency begets an even weaker currency. These cycles are prominent in emerging markets history. Really big currency moves are always an indication something is happening that's worth understanding.

Don't Fear Too Much Debt—Fear Bad Debt

Another legacy of the crisis—too much debt—is often misunderstood by investors. Repeatedly, debt is denounced as evil without distinction between *good* and *bad* debt. Debt acquired in a financially responsible manner to grow and invest is an ancient practice and a good one—it fuels economic dynamism. We don't criticize Wal-Mart for taking on debt; it wouldn't be where it is today without it. Bad debt, on the other hand, *is* bad: It's acquired inappropriately, put to inefficient use, prohibitively expensive, and so on. This is the stuff carried by banks during the Asian Financial Crisis and should be a warning to investors.

Massive Currency Reserves

Capital flows were beneficial to economic development, but the crisis showed how vulnerable countries were to sudden reversals. Governments thus realized the need for greater currency reserves to promote stability. As Figure 2.3 shows, emerging market governments (and not just Asian) embarked on a massive accumulation of reserves over the next decade. China stands out—its reserve holdings dwarf all other countries because of its massive trade surplus. But other countries increased reserves at an even faster rate. Russia, for example, holds

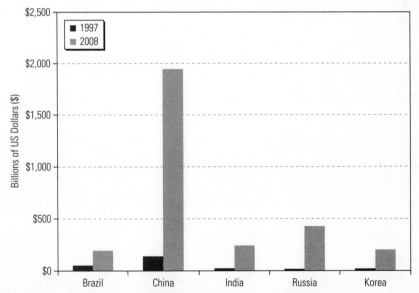

Figure 2.3   Foreign Currency Reserves: 1997 vs. 2008
Source: Thomson Datastream.

over 24 times more in 2008 than a decade earlier. As of this writing, a new financial crisis is unfolding, with many of the same currency pressures as the Asian Financial Crisis. This time around, many emerging markets have leaned on these reserves to maintain stability.

THE DRAGON UNLEASHED

China's economic history is an ancient one—stories of Marco Polo and the Spice Route have captured the imagination of scholars and historians alike for centuries. Opening a newspaper or turning on the television today has the same effect, with enthusiastic stories of its economic might. Indeed, China has rapidly ascended the global economic food chain in the past several decades. But often lost amid the awe: The Chinese stock market is a relatively new creation—underdeveloped, plagued by structural inefficiencies, and subject to the whims of an often heavy-handed government. This clashes with popular perception, leaving investors with a clouded view of China's role in the global capital markets.

Deng and the Birth of the Modern Chinese Economy

Modern Chinese history begins in 1949. That year, the Communist Party of China (CPC) led by Mao Zedong ended a bitter civil war lasting over two decades, establishing the People's Republic of China, as it's known today. For the next three decades, Chairman Mao led China through a series of economic reforms based on communist principles. In hindsight, these reforms impeded economic progress more than they helped, and Mao's policies had virtually nothing to do with turning China into the economic powerhouse it is today.[24] In fact, it was his death in 1976 that truly marked the birth of the modern Chinese economy.

A struggle for power followed Mao's death, and in 1978, Deng Xiaoping wrestled control from Mao's designated successor. Deng's rise to power was a critical turning point for the country. Under Mao's rule, China's economy was crippled by the collectivist principles of communism. Deng's model, aptly named *gaige kaifang* (literally, "reforms and openness"), offered an escape. His goals were unique—paradoxical even—to the communist way. Deng tried to reconcile capitalism's belief in free markets with Marxism-Leninism views on central planning, a model often referred to today as "market socialism."

Deng recognized the path to economic prosperity involved liberating the creative energies of the people and allowing market forces to prevail. Communist communes were disbanded. Peasants and farmers were allowed to lease the land they worked on for as long as 30 years. Families were required to pay a certain quantity of goods to the state at a fixed price for their rent, but they were openly allowed to sell anything beyond that in free markets. Deng also endorsed an "open door" policy of economic engagement with the rest of the world. He let in foreign capital, technology, and expertise.

Though the spirit of these reforms suggests eager progress toward the adoption of free market values, the Chinese system at the time was still a long way away from what we call capitalism. The state still dominated key cogs of the economy (and maintained a stranglehold on politics). But it was a system that could at least get along with the increasingly capitalistic world outside its borders.

In fact, in some ways the new Chinese model was a remarkably effective method of economic organization. By definition, democratic nations need consensus to pass laws or adopt economic reforms. China, on the other hand, could use its state-controlled machine to force through whatever it wished. Such political authoritarianism meant life could still be brutal, but the economic results were undeniable. The economy boomed under Deng, growing at an average annualized pace of 9.9 percent from 1981 to 1989.[25] China was no longer an afterthought, but a nation finally beginning to flex its economic muscles on the global stage.

Growth Takes Off

It wasn't until shortly after official retirement, however, that Deng scored his coup de grace. During his now-famous "southern tour" in 1992, Deng ceremoniously traveled to southern provinces. In various speeches throughout his tour, he urged the population to "be a little bolder, go a little faster," and roused support for his visions of economic reform and openness.[26] Deng's speeches lit off a firecracker of activity—the economy expanded 14.2 percent in 1992 and 14.0 percent in 1993.

By the mid-1990s, China was an unstoppable force not even the Asian Financial Crisis could derail. Despite Deng's open-door policy, China hadn't yet intertwined itself with the rest of the world quite like other East Asian nations. It had a closed capital account (meaning no money could flow *out* of the country), didn't rely on foreign debt, and the state still played a dominant role in the country's financial flows. Growth slowed somewhat due to the follies of its neighbors—to a low of 7.6 percent in 1999—but it was hardly a catastrophic slowdown.[27]

Following the crisis, China resumed its torrid pace of growth. By now, it was the world's manufacturing center, offering abundant cheap labor. Trade with the rest of the world exploded. Exports rose from $52 billion in 1989 to $1.2 *trillion* in 2007. China's thirst for the world's goods was equally impressive, rising from around $60 billion to nearly $1 trillion over the same period.[28] To put the sheer scale of this rise in perspective, consider China's combined exports and imports were larger than Italy's *entire* economy in 2007.[29]

But it wasn't just trade—the scale and speed of investment were also unprecedented. According to the *Economist*, from 2001 to 2005, more was spent on roads, railways, and other fixed assets than was spent in the previous 50 years. Between 2006 and 2010, $200 billion is expected to be invested in railways alone, as the country ambitiously lays down 75,000 miles of track in the world's largest railway expansion since the US transcontinental line in the 1860s.[30] Gross capital formation, a broad proxy for overall investment, averaged 15 percent annual growth in the 12 years ending in 2007, from $250 billion to $1.3 trillion.[31]

Years of strong economic growth also dramatically lifted wealth, leading to a burgeoning middle class with money to spend and increasingly expensive tastes. With over a billion people, the Chinese consumer became a coveted end market.

These developments are rightly intoxicating to investors. China's economic growth story is unlike anything most of us will ever see in our lifetimes. Not surprisingly, investors hone in on these credentials as proof the country offers the opportunity of a lifetime. Unfortunately, structural impediments created by the country's political model mean its economic accomplishments don't necessarily translate to investment reality.

THE HISTORY OF CHINA'S STOCK MARKET— A LESSON IN SUPPLY AND DEMAND

It's common for investors to correlate economic strength with positive markets (or a slow-growing economy to market weakness). A fast-growing economy implies healthy economic developments, and markets should reflect that by moving upward, right? Meanwhile, slowing growth raises recessionary fears, and markets should be correspondingly spooked. Makes sense! Except it's not quite right. Economic events may impact market fundamentals or sway sentiment, but they are not the primary drivers behind market performance—ultimately supply and demand for securities are. China's capital market history is a textbook example of how distortions in the supply and demand of equities can render macroeconomic analysis moot for investors.

A Brief History of Chinese Market Returns

Relative even to some of its emerging market peers, China's stock market is a recent creation. It was born December 1990 with two exchanges— the Shanghai Stock Exchange and Shenzhen Stock Exchange. (The market had been disbanded with Mao's rise to power in 1949.)

Table 2.3 shows annual stock market returns for the Shanghai Stock Exchange Composite since inception. Early trading was massively bullish. In 1991 and 1992, the first data available, the composite rose over 500 percent! Markets took a breather in 1994 and 1995, but they took off once again the following year and rose fairly consistently through 2000. It was by all accounts a rewarding time to be in Chinese stocks. An investor who bought $1,000 worth of Chinese shares in 1991 would have had nearly $16,000 10 years later.[32]

Table 2.3   Shanghai Stock Exchange
Composite Returns

1991	129.4%	2000	51.7%
1992	166.6%	2001	−20.6%
1993	6.8%	2002	−17.5%
1994	−22.3%	2003	10.3%
1995	−14.3%	2004	−15.4%
1996	65.1%	2005	−8.3%
1997	30.2%	2006	130.4%
1998	−4.0%	2007	96.7%
1999	19.2%	2008	−65.4%

Source: Global Financial Data.

But all bull markets come to an end. In 2001, the market turned abruptly downward, entering a vicious bear market. By the close of 2005, the Shanghai Stock Exchange had lost nearly half its value. Markets rebounded dramatically in 2006, kicking off another massive bull market. In 2007, markets had yet another incredible year, returning 97 percent.

What was the Chinese economy doing all this time? Surely following the up and down fluctuations of the market, right? Hardly— it powered ahead as if nothing had changed. While equities cycled through boom and bust, the economy averaged over 10 percent growth a year.[33] But if the economy wasn't behind the market, what was?

The Supply and Demand of Equities

Stocks are like anything else bought and sold in a free market—prices are determined by *supply* and *demand*. In the short term, stocks are primarily driven by demand. Why? Demand can change almost instantaneously. A single earnings release, management change, or shift in the macroeconomic climate can quickly change investment demand.

The supply of stocks, on the other hand, isn't so malleable. New stocks usually come to market via initial public offerings (IPOs) or secondary offerings—which don't happen overnight. Investment bankers and corporate executives see when a particular category is getting hot, and they join in on the fun by issuing shares too. This process takes time and, because demand is high, prices keep rising. The more prices rise, the more supply is created.

Eventually supply, or the anticipation of more of it, outpaces demand. Either there are no more buyers or prices just get too high and demand can't grow fast enough to keep up—and thus prices fall, sometimes dramatically. Look back no further than the beginning of the millennium to see this cycle at work. In the first quarter of 2000, there was an average of four public stock offerings every trading day in the US alone. Globally, there were over 13 offerings per day![34] What does this have to do with Chinese stocks?

The Curious Case of Chinese A-Shares

When China's stock exchanges were introduced in the early 1990s, only a small portion of each company's outstanding shares was made tradeable, or *floated*, as "A-shares." The other two-thirds represented interests of the state and were non-tradeable, presumably so the government could maintain control over them.

Float

A company's *float* refers to the percentage of its shares freely tradeable on the open market. It may surprise you that many major companies do not freely float all of their shares. For example, nearly a third of Wal-Mart's shares are owned by the Walton family and thus not available on the open market. In the case of many emerging market companies, the government is often a major stakeholder.

One can easily imagine how this would distort the market's natural pricing mechanism. With only a small percentage of outstanding shares available to the public, equities soon began to trade on their scarcity value, not fundamentals. The government exacerbated the situation by declaring the non-tradeable shares would never be sold into the open market.[35] This meant market participants could effectively take supply out of the equation. With this constrained supply and strong demand, prices went higher and higher. This largely drove the big market run-up throughout the 1990s.

Supply Fears Feed the Bear

By the turn of the decade, however, the government began to reconsider the existing share structure. It understood such restrictions interfered with its original intention of modernizing companies through stock market listings. As such, the government began discussing possible mechanisms to float state-owned shares. In 2001, China's security regulator made an announcement the market interpreted as a sign the government would allow the full float of the shares without any compensation to exiting shareholders.

Investors hate uncertainty, and markets nosedived as the rumor spread. Chinese officials were slow to react to the problem, and fears of massive dilution from the government's supply of state-owned shares continued to weigh on equities for the next several years. It was the fear of this supply overhang that primarily drove the five-year bear market from 2001 to 2005.

Share Reform Unleashes the Bull

By mid-2005, the Chinese government rolled out a plan to convert non-tradeable state shares into freely tradeable ones. While details varied across firms, the share-conversion program dictated that existing A-share holders be compensated for the dilution of their shares and, more importantly, that the converted state-owned shares be "locked up" for three years. This effectively meant the state-owned shares would remain untradeable for at least another three years. For all intents and purposes, the status quo was maintained.

The lifting of uncertainty had predictable results. Now assured there would be no state-owned share supply dump in the near future, investors rushed back into Chinese stocks. At one point in 2007, over a million new Chinese brokerage accounts were opened a week; and in May, trading volumes exceeded the rest of Asia *combined.*[36]

As would be expected, bankers were itching to get to work. They got their wish in 2006 when the government reopened IPO markets (they had been temporarily banned since the start of share reform in 2005), letting loose a share-issuing frenzy. Nearly \$65 billion in new shares was listed in 2007 alone, a 280 percent increase in the amount offered in 2006.[37]

Capital Controls and the Demand Side

So far we have only mentioned supply, but demand can also be artificially manipulated. China's capital account is closed, meaning Chinese citizens are not allowed to invest directly abroad. The government offers a few programs that allow mutual funds to invest internationally, but the quotas remain relatively small and stringent. The Chinese are mostly stuck investing in local markets. Moreover, since China's bond market is underdeveloped and shallow, investors are forced into either hard assets (such as real estate or gold), equities, or cash. It logically follows that demand for equities would be artificially high in such a scenario. We can see this at work in the pricing differences between two types of Chinese shares, but first, some definitions.

Alphabet Soup of Shares   Because of its closed capital account, there are several types of Chinese shares available.

- **A-Shares.** The primary mainland Chinese listing. A-shares are available only to *domestic* Chinese investors.
- **B-Shares.** B-shares are also listed on the mainland stock exchanges, but were originally the exact opposite of A-shares—available only to *foreign* investors. However, in 2001 the government opened B-shares to mainland residents. The B-share market is notably smaller and less liquid than the A-share market.
- **H-Shares.** Chinese companies listed on the Hong Kong Stock Exchange. Hong Kong is a special administrative region under the

sovereignty of mainland China, but has a separate government and markets are unencumbered by Chinese restrictions.
- **S-Shares.** Chinese companies listed on Singapore's exchange.

The A-Share and H-Share Premium   For the most part, investors follow two markets—the A-shares and the H-shares. A-shares represent the domestic Chinese stock market and are subject to the capital controls discussed previously. H-shares are owned by pretty much everyone else, including institutional and retail investors from all over the globe.

There are many companies that list on *both* exchanges to tap demand from domestic and foreign investors. Since these shares represent the *same* company, it should follow that its price movements are roughly the same too, right? Wrong. Only domestic Chinese investors can buy A-shares. But foreign investors can buy shares *anywhere*, in any country, not just H-shares. H-shares thus reflect the demand for Chinese companies by global investors as a whole, while A-shares represent the supply-constrained Chinese investor.

Hang Seng Indexes, an index provider in the region, produces the AH Premium Index, which measures the absolute price premium

Figure 2.4   Hang Seng China AH Premium Index
Source: Thomson Datastream, Bloomberg Finance L.P.

(or discount) of A-shares over H-shares for the same companies (see Figure 2.4). As you can see, A-shares consistently cost more, sometimes 100 percent more, than their H-share peers! This is because demand for A-shares is artificially higher from the capital controls. Were capital allowed to freely flow, these discrepancies would likely be virtually nonexistent.

The Government as Ultimate Arbiter

The supply and demand of equities isn't the only thing the Chinese government controls. The vast role of the state in the economy also means traditional fundamental drivers are often irrelevant.

Consider an example. You may recall the impressive statistics on railway construction—75,000 miles of track is expected to be laid by 2020. It will be the largest high-speed passenger network on Earth. If you operate a railroad company, your prospects aren't likely to get much brighter than that, right?

Not when you're a Chinese railroad company—the government has its say first. China's Ministry of Railways maintains majority control over all rail tracks, setting rates for farm products and ticket prices for migrant workers at artificially low prices to appease the vast rural population. One estimate put the Ministry's net profit margin at less than 1 percent of revenues of $35 billion.[38] Maybe that doesn't sound like such a great investment after all.

These examples exist across all segments of the Chinese market, not just railroad companies. The government has its hand in virtually every aspect of the economy and market. As such, winners and losers are often determined directly by the government, not the free market. This model is another reason why general optimism over the country's prospects doesn't necessarily lead to smart investment decisions.

Lessons and Legacies

Even though China's stock market history is relatively short, it offers three very important lessons to investors:

1. **Don't confuse economics with markets.** While strong equity returns sometimes correlate with a rapidly growing economy, it isn't a necessary condition.

2. **Look for structural factors affecting the market.** Many times structural factors can trump fundamentals. Investors should be aware of how these factors may impact a country's equity markets, and, if they exist, look to foreign companies that may have exposure to the country's economics but not the structural impediments.

3. **Be wary of government.** There is no getting around government meddling in equity markets, and it is especially egregious in emerging markets. Where possible, choose investments where markets, not the government, are the primary price arbiter.

Chapter Recap

The East Asian "miracle" captivated the investing public in the mid-1990s—many saw the world's economic gravity tipping eastward and markets correspondingly soared.

- Much of this strong performance stemmed from sound policy decisions and positive reform implemented by Asian governments in decades prior.
- But the Asian Financial Crisis quickly changed the prevailing optimism.
  - Currency devaluation in Thailand triggered a crisis that ripped through the region, leaving markets decimated and entire economies on the brink of collapse.
  - The crisis exposed massive levels of foreign currency borrowing and the inefficiencies of government-directed lending, taking some of the gleam off the boom of the previous decades.
  - Policymakers learned key lessons, stockpiling reserves to guard against future calamity and taking a more conservative view on debt.
- Investors may find China's siren song too difficult to resist, but its role in global capital markets is often misunderstood.
  - While the country's economic track record is impressive, investors too often confuse economic prowess with stock market outperformance.
  - Instead, China teaches us the importance of supply and demand in capital markets pricing—perhaps the most valuable lesson to any investor.

3

LATIN AMERICA AND THE VAGARIES OF BOOM AND BUST

Latin America is a land rich in opportunity. It was once a "new world," mystifying European settlers with powerful symbols of wealth, technology, and culture. Its fertile lands held the promise of abundant natural resources, both agricultural and industrial. Capitalism also has a rich history here, from pre-colonial trade to the coffee barons of nineteenth-century Brazil to burgeoning financial services today.

Yet, for all its allure, Latin America is a region defined by contradiction, of promise and change mitigated by bouts of boom and bust. For decades, Latin American countries witnessed currency crises, bank failures, hyperinflation—a violent cascade of every conceivable economic disaster. The region's long history with populism has exacerbated this tumultuous past. Rightly or wrongly, it is viewed as the "basket case" of emerging markets.

Despite these flaws, Latin America's siren song has often proved too hard to resist. Just when it appears investments in the region should be shunned forever, recovery restores hope anew and investors flock again to its shores. Given Latin America's vast, resource-rich potential, this is justified. But an understanding of its deeply cyclical past is a crucial prerequisite for emerging markets investors. With this in mind, we chronicle the last few decades of Latin America's tumultuous history, starting with its often unique relationship between politics and economics.

THE POLITICAL ECONOMY OF LATIN AMERICA

The adventures of Dorothy, Toto, the Scarecrow, the Tin Woodman, and the Lion in the classic fairy tale *The Wonderful Wizard of Oz* captivated imaginations for generations. It is a magical story of yellow brick roads, rainbows, witches, and, of course, a wizard. As endearing as these images are, Lyman Frank Baum's novel, published in 1900, represented much more. Hidden within the memorable characters and storylines were strong allegorical references to the then-tumultuous state of US politics.

At the end of the nineteenth century, rural farmers revolted in the US. Tired of their perceived oppression by Eastern industrialists and bankers, the farmers united to challenge the existing establishment, forming the Populist Party. The party represented the interests of these hard-working, "common" folk and called for the end of big government and the return of power to the people.

Powerful symbols from this era appear throughout Baum's novel. Kansas was the birthplace of the Populist Party in 1892—and of Dorothy. The Munchkins were imprisoned by the Wicked Witch of the East, much like the farmers believed they were imprisoned by financial interests and the government. The Scarecrow, Tin Woodman, and Lion were all symbols. Every time the Tin Woodman swung an ax, he chopped off a different part of his body, to be replaced by Oz tinsmiths. Soon he was entirely made of tin and without a heart—like the Easterners turning a hard-working, common man into a heartless machine.[1] Baum's novel thus became synonymous with the history of the Populist Party and its ideologies, known as *populism*.

What does Dorothy have to do with Latin America? Populism has taken many forms in various places and times, but it is closely associated with Latin America's political history. Virtually every country

in the region has at least briefly experimented with the model, impart-
ing a profound legacy on its economy and markets.

Populism and Latin America

A precise definition of populism is difficult to pin down. It's taken
many guises in Latin America—authoritarian and intolerant in Brazil
under President Getúlio Vargas, but more democratic and moderate
in Peru's political experiments. However, the underlying ethos is essentially the same. Edwin Williamson, author of *The Penguin History of
Latin America*, describes it well:

> . . . [Populism is] the phenomenon whereby a politician tries to
> win power by courting mass popularity with sweeping promises
> of benefits and concessions to large interest-groups, usually drawn
> from the lower classes. Populist leaders lack a coherent programme
> for social change or economic reform, but try to manipulate the
> existing system in order to lavish favours on underprivileged sec-
> tors in return for their support.[2]

As Williamson alludes, populism is about people—the word itself
is derived from the Latin word *populus*, meaning precisely that. Both
politically and economically, populism has come to mean policies
driven by and for "the people," and populist episodes often arise with
the disaffection of a group and their desire to reclaim some form of
"ownership" over society and government.

This estrangement is a recurring theme in Latin American history.
The region has long suffered from inequality. The second half of the
nineteenth century saw the rise of a powerful export oligarchy. They
were capitalists only in the sense that they looked to profit from selling
goods into the market. But they prospered largely from their political
connections and monopolistic stranglehold on industry. Their success meant a small group of elites held a high concentration of income
and assets. The sharp class and sectoral divisions developed between
these wealthy asset holders and the lower-middle class workers can
still be felt today. By one measure of income inequality—the Gini
coefficient—Latin America remains the world's most unequal region.[3]

Populism represented a natural alternative to this oligarchic past—a voice for the common man long suppressed by vested interests. In modern times, politicians have shrewdly catered to the alienated lower class to attain political power, leading to a number of key policies with profound implications for investors.

Later in the chapter, we provide an illustration of populism in practice under Brazilian president José Sarney in the mid- to late 1980s. Sarney's populist bent was one reason for the country's slow recovery from the 1982 debt crisis. But first, we summarize some of the most impactful legacies for investors from this political model, as these transcend any particular populist episode.

Fiscal Policy

All democratic governments are to some degree beholden to the groups that provide their electoral victory. For Latin America's populists, that was the increasingly disenchanted and disadvantaged lower class. Progress largely bypassed this segment of society, and to win their support, politicians offered promises of monetary handouts and concessions. In practice, this translated to profligate fiscal spending on welfare and social initiatives—often beyond the revenue means of the government (i.e., *deficit* spending). Effectively, the government takes the economy on its shoulders and spends its way to growth.

Most populist governments are able to stimulate expansion for a short period of time with such policy. But eventually the government must source additional funds to continue supporting fiscal spending, since cutting these policies is political suicide. This uncovers two key themes found throughout Latin American history: high levels of monetary growth and a long-running love affair with debt and foreign capital. Both contribute substantially to the instability often associated with Latin American populist regimes.

The Scourge of Inflation

Undisciplined fiscal spending often leads populist governments to hijack the money printing press, and the ensuing excessive monetary growth in turn creates inflationary pressures. Why is this so? As the famous US economist Milton Friedman once said: "Inflation is always and everywhere a monetary phenomenon."[4] This means inflation is a function of liquidity—money supply—relative to the real economic demand for money. When money creation is in excess of total output growth, it invariably leads to inflation.

We can see this clearly in Latin America's history. The political concessions and handouts associated with populist regimes meant money was not always flowing through to the most productive economic hands. Total output growth was often substantially less than the growth of money, creating excess liquidity. And, more consistently than any other region in the world, Latin America has been afflicted by the scourge of inflation. Brazil represents one of the most egregious examples. Between 1980 and 1994, inflation increased an average of more than 100 percent per year. Put another way, prices increased by a total of 166 *billion* percent over the course of those 15 years.[5] That's an unfathomably large number.

Inflation approaching such levels is called *hyperinflation*. But it doesn't have to get even nearly that far to incite instability. High inflation causes real incomes to decline, reducing consumption power. Lenders are also penalized because the real amount borrowers repay is less, hindering investment. For stocks, it reduces the present value of future earnings. If unchecked long enough, the decline in real incomes can become substantial enough to foster social unrest as the price of staple goods reaches stratospheric levels. The devastation of hyper-inflationary periods is evident throughout history—from Germany's Weimar republic in the 1920s to Zimbabwe today.

Too-high inflation also distorts important price signals between producers, businesses, and consumers. A higher price for a pencil, to borrow from Friedman again, usually indicates people want more of it and that more resources should be employed to produce and meet the increase in demand. But in times of high inflation, companies may mistake the increased price of the pencil for an increase in demand when it really is a function of the inflation-related adjustments to prices (or vice versa). As you can imagine, a well-run business would likely slow production in the face of such uncertainty—it doesn't want to produce more of a product people don't want. Eventually, this leads to shortages.

A little inflation is a good thing, however. In fact, the worst possible price environment is one of declining prices, or *deflation*, where nominal wages and profits fall while the real debt burden increases. Borrowers are thus forced to reduce spending or, even worse, default. If you still think falling prices is a good thing, look at Japan's economic stagnation throughout the 1990s.

Property Rights and Wealth Redistribution

Markets are inextricably linked to political models. And political models are as varied as the cultures and people governed by them— democracy, authoritarianism, communism, populism, socialism, pick an -ism! Politics, through legislation, regulation, or even diktat, set the rules of the game. This is crucially important to investors—these models play a large role in determining winners and losers.

Depending on your -ism, the rules of the game can be substantially different. For instance, economic policies under Latin America's populist states benefited the lower-middle class (at least at first), and wealthy asset holders were the losers. By contrast, the winners in a democratic state are individuals motivated enough to compete for such status. Here, individual liberty generally sets people free to find their own success. Thus, while politics may enforce the rules, the model itself is equally critical—it determines what the rules *are*.

These rules also mean different things to different actors in the economy. The local butcher providing you with Sunday's pot roast will be affected by the political framework quite differently than the electric utility company supplying the power to the light you may be using to read this book. For example, in the US, the Food and Drug Administration has little impact on the profitability of your local utility company, but it clearly governs the actions of the butcher.

It's through this framework investors should evaluate the relationship between markets and politics. In Latin America, both directly and indirectly, the government's populist policies rested on wealth redistribution. Appeasing the masses meant taking from the "haves" and giving to the "have-nots." This included redistributing land, subsidizing prices for select consumer goods and companies, or subsidizing incomes, among others. Winners and losers were determined not by market forces, but by the motivations of the populist politicians.

Markets generally abhor forced redistributive policies. Basic property rights, protections, and contract enforcement are critical to the proper functioning of markets. Consider a simple example: A local drug company spends several years developing a drug that shows promising signs of reversing Alzheimer's disease. It spent several hundred million dollars on the drug's development, knowing it has a superb chance of being a blockbuster when it reaches the market. In the US, such an investment would be protected under patent law. But what if there were no such protection? Think the drug company would still expend such time and money on its development? Not on your life. Markets—and their profit opportunities—drive economic innovations and progress. Redistributive policy stifles this by injecting uncertainty and disincentives to take on risk for potential profit.

More Volatile Cycles

Last, from a broader perspective, many of the policies inherent in populist regimes—undisciplined fiscal spending, runaway inflation, a lack of property rights—contribute to substantially more volatile and pronounced market cycles. In the "typical" Latin American recession within the period of 1970 to 1994, output fell by an average 8 percent. In the OECD countries—a group of 30 rich, developed markets—it fell by 2 percent.[6] A similar trend appears in the stock market. Based on annual returns since 1988, Latin America is 30 percent more volatile than emerging markets as a whole.[7] Several of these episodes stand out, and the remainder of this chapter will be devoted to better understanding their significance.

TILL DEBT DO US PART—THE 1982 CRISIS

On August 12, 1982, Mexico shook the world when the country's finance minister announced it would be unable to meet its August 16 interest payment on over $80 billion in mainly US dollar-denominated debt.

The country effectively declared default on its international obligations, but Mexico's plight was far from an isolated phenomenon. News
of Mexico's default awoke investors to the massive level of indebtedness
across all of Latin America—the total outstanding debt for the region at
year end 1982 was $332 billion.[8] Brazil alone owed $87.5 billion, the
largest single debt for one country at the time.[9]

Soon investors realized this was not just a Latin American crisis,
either. The debt's source was a tangled web of loans linking the global
banking system—from Chicago to London to Tokyo. Mexico's default
thus triggered global concerns of a systemic collapse.

Yet its epicenter remained in Latin America. The sheer size of its
debt burden would weigh on the region for a long time—the 1980s are
known as the "lost decade" in Latin America. How did this happen?
The origins of Latin America's love affair with debt may surprise you.
It began with a series of distinct, seemingly unrelated events following
World War II.

The Set Up

In the aftermath of World War II, the US assumed a dominant role in
reshaping the world order. The Marshall Plan sent hundreds of millions
of dollars to Europe to rebuild after the devastation of war. Meanwhile,
an age of consumerism took hold in the US, and Americans developed
a thirst for imported goods from around the globe. As a result, US dollars in global circulation increased markedly. Foreign companies often
kept this currency in the custody of their local bank, but other countries held the monies in US-domiciled financial institutions.

This was also the start of the Cold War, and the Soviet Union
didn't trust US banks. It had good reason—during the war, the US
government impounded Soviet dollar holdings. Yet Soviet officials
didn't wish to surrender their dollar claims. Seeking alternatives, they
found a British bank willing to offer US dollar deposits. This suited
the Soviets. The bank was not domiciled in the US and thus not
subject to its banking laws—the money was beyond the reach of US
authorities. The arrangement was also agreeable to the British bank.

It could take Russia's dollar deposits, turn around, and lend it some-where else. Along with other minor precursors, this would soon put what was called the Eurodollar market on the map.

The Eurodollar market—comprised of a network of international banks—facilitates this very simple function: Providing access to US dollars outside of the US. Banks domiciled around the world can access short-term US dollar financing through the Eurodollar market. Today, it is one of the largest international capital markets.

Surging Oil Prices

What does the Eurodollar market's rise have to do with Latin America? Oil!

In 1973, the Organization of Petroleum Exporting Countries (OPEC) cut production and placed an embargo on its oil exports. The US and the Netherlands were targeted in particular (the Arab world was retaliating their decision to supply arms to Israel in the Yom Kippur War), but the entire world was dramatically impacted. At the time, OPEC provided just over 50 percent of the world's oil supply.[10] Not surprisingly, oil prices shot through the roof from the dramatic reduction in supply—increasing 237 percent in January 1974 alone.[11] Oil prices jumped again in 1979 when the Iranian Revolution shuttered Iranian oil exports and set off a global oil panic. That year, prices rose nearly 150 percent[12](see Figure 3.1).

Oil-exporting nations found themselves flush with cash as a result of the price increases. Between 1972 and 1974, OPEC's annual oil

Embargo

An *embargo* is the conscious policy decision by one country to completely block trade with another country. Embargoes are usually politically motivated and, because they bring trade to a standstill, are the most aggressive of all trade barriers. In comparison, tariffs or taxes merely decrease levels of trade. The most well-known example in recent memory is the US embargo on Cuba in 1960.

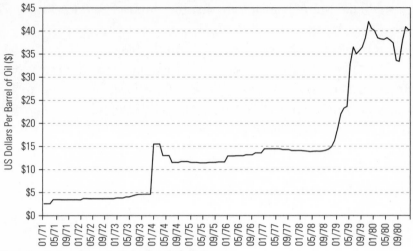

Figure 3.1   Brent Crude Oil Prices

Source: Global Financial Data.

revenues jumped from $14 billion to nearly $70 billion. By 1977, they had nearly doubled again to $128 billion.[13] This was more money than these nations could possibly consume, so their current account surpluses grew quite large. Where did this money end up? That's right, the Eurodollar market. By 1978, OPEC had approximately $84 billion in bank deposits, mostly in the Eurodollar market.[14]

If rising oil prices led to current account surpluses in oil-exporting nations, the opposite must also be true: Current account deficits exist in oil-importing nations. High oil prices were a boon to those countries fortunate enough to have an abundant source of "black gold," but the rising cost of oil imports meant countries on the other side of the fence were correspondingly worse off. Many Latin American countries fit this bill. Combined with the social welfare spending associated with populist governments, the region saw its deficits grow, leaving it in need of funds.

Tapping a New Source

Up to this point, emerging market nations had largely relied on other governments or international organizations for funds. But developed country governments were hesitant to lend at the time—they had

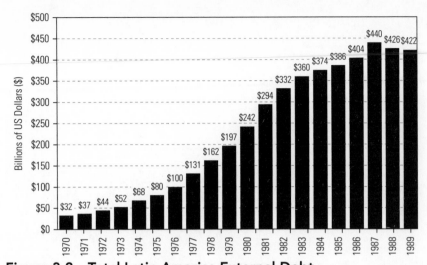

Figure 3.2   Total Latin America External Debt

Source: The World Bank Group. Data are based on the Latin America & Caribbean group as defined by the World Bank.

their own problems.[15] Borrowing from oil-rich countries was also not politically viable—these countries profited for the same reason Latin America suffered.

Latin America tapped into another source—the Eurodollar market. Commercial banks across the globe were happy to provide funds to Latin American governments. Banks saw little risk in passing on credit to these countries. The common parlance at the time was "governments don't go bankrupt." The growth in lending over the next decade was staggering: Major international banks increased their loans to Latin America at an average rate of 30 percent a year for 10 years.[16]

Throughout the 1970s, the region devoured this recycled oil money. Figure 3.2 illustrates the magnitude. The rate and scale of Latin America's debt accumulation was unmatched—by the early 1980s, the debt burden had jumped well over $300 billion.

Debt Complications

Given the sheer size of the debt accumulated, the ability to service it became a critical variable. By 1982, Latin America was paying nearly 50 percent of export earnings to service its debt, with some countries, like Brazil, forking over even more. Bankers generally considered 30 percent an acceptable level.[17] Foreign capital inflows turned to mild outflows around this time, as investors worried debt levels had approached unsustainable levels.

Debt Service Burden

Imagine taking out a mortgage on your most recent property purchase. To most people, the overall amount of the loan is beyond what anyone could pay in a reasonable time-frame—that's why they make 30-*year* mortgages! But the most important thing to the bank (and you) is your ability to make monthly payments. As long as you're consistently making these, both parties are happy.

Your *debt service burden* would be your monthly payments divided by some measure of income or assets—it's a tool to measure how likely you can meet your obligations. For a country, some other similar measure of income is used, such as gross domestic product or export earnings. As the total debt load increases, the debtor's ability to meet payments also becomes more difficult—its debt service burden is increasing. While the level is subjective, there is a point where it gets too high. We can see this at work in Latin America toward the end of the 1970s and into the 1980s.

Matters were complicated by an additional factor. Approximately two-thirds of the debt accumulated paid variable rates, meaning the interest rate reset periodically. In this case, the rate was tied to the London Interbank Offering Rate (LIBOR) and reset every six months or so.[18] LIBOR is the rate quoted by European banks to borrow US dollars on the Eurodollar market (the cost to borrow dollars outside of the US). In a relatively benign interest rate environment this wasn't an issue. But it left Latin American countries subject to macroeconomic conditions outside their borders.

The "Lost Decade"

Those conditions worsened materially toward the end of the 1970s. The decade's second oil shock sent US inflation soaring—prices rose

Figure 3.3   US 90-Day Treasury Bill Yields
Source: Global Financial Data.

by 13 percent in 1979, a very high rate for a developed country.[19] In August 1979, President Jimmy Carter appointed Paul Volcker head of the Federal Reserve. Intent on crushing inflation, Volcker raised interest rates higher than any other time in modern US history. Rates on three-month Treasury bills soared above 17 percent in 1980 (see Figure 3.3).[20]

Volcker successfully tamed inflation—prices rose only 4 percent in 1982—but his actions were not without consequences. His aggressive monetary policy helped push the US into a deep recession, which soon reverberated throughout the globe.

Higher interest rates and slow growth were a double whammy to Latin America. Since their LIBOR debt was tied to US interest rates, servicing costs immediately spiked. At the same time, slower growth left governments with less revenue to meet the expanding payments. The situation worsened quickly—countries took on additional debt solely to make interest rate payments on existing debt, a veritable Ponzi scheme. Such a situation was untenable and destined to collapse.

And collapse it did in August 1982, with Mexico's announcement it couldn't meet its scheduled interest rate payment. Mexico was in a precarious situation. Not only was the government smarting from higher

Ponzi Scheme

In 1921, Charles Ponzi told investors he could provide a 40 percent return in just 90 days through buying and selling international mail coupons. This was quite an enticing option at a time when bank savings accounts yielded 5 percent. His offer was hard to resist—he collected over $1 million in one three-hour period. He paid the first few investors to appear legitimate, but his scheme soon unraveled. It was later discovered Ponzi had only purchased $30 of coupons. Today, *Ponzi schemes* generally refer to instances where the money from new investors is used to pay old investors. For a detailed discussion on how to spot these types of frauds, see Ken Fisher's *How to Smell a Rat: The Five Signs of Financial Fraud.*

Source: US Securities and Exchange Commission, "Ponzi Schemes," (April 19, 2001).

interest rates, but revenues from oil, a major export, also fell with the global recession and sharp decline in oil prices that year. Mexico's default quickly rippled through to other debt-laden developing countries. By year end, nearly 40 nations were in arrears on their debt.[21]

These bad loans had infected the entire global banking sector. At the end of 1985, global commercial banks had lent $217 billion, with US banks holding 42 percent of the loans; European banks, 37 percent; and Canadian banks, 8 percent. In the US alone, the nine largest banks made loans to these countries equal to 233 percent of their primary capital.[22] Latin America's default had the potential to bring the world's financial system to its knees.

Wrong Diagnosis, Wrong Prescription

The scale and interconnectedness of the crisis snapped the developed world to attention. Governments and international organizations used every resource available—from swap lines to the Bank of International Settlements loans (the central bank of central banks)—to prevent a global financial collapse. By the end of 1982, the situation had cooled—the world wasn't coming to an end. The US economy began to show signs of recovery, and officials breathed a little easier. But while the initial response was coordinated and quick, policy responses in the next several years were too timid and failed to spur the necessary reforms for complete recovery.

Policymakers initially viewed the crisis as one of liquidity, not solvency. Officials believed the fundamental health of the troubled countries was largely sound, but that they were shut out of international capital markets. That is, Latin American governments couldn't pay their debt because investors were too scared to give them money. Developed market nations, especially the US, were therefore against forgiving any part of the debt and pushed for postponement instead. The initial policy response gave Latin American governments enough loans to service their debt, requiring IMF-like austerity measures to resuscitate economic growth. These measures included tax and tariff increases and a prescription to reduce spending. If growth successfully returned, so too would investors and the necessary liquidity—or so the theory went.

Unfortunately, this was equivalent to using painkillers to treat an infection. It masked the pain but did little to cure the underlying problem. Troubled governments were largely able to meet payments with the additional loans, but austerity measures did little to invigorate growth, let alone attract foreign investors.

It was clear after a few years this solution was ineffective. The prospects of a return by investors seemed dim, and debt levels continued to rise (see Figure 3.2). In 1985, US Treasury Secretary James A. Baker introduced a new plan offering $9 billion from multilateral agencies and $20 billion from commercial banks in exchange for market-based reforms. Many of these reforms were different from those first proposed: tax cuts, a reduction of trade barriers, and the privatization of state companies. But the plan still included no forgiveness—policymakers remained staunchly in favor of postponing the debt. The Baker Plan was thus of a similar vein as the previous efforts.

By the end of the decade, it became clear the Baker Plan was also a failure. Developed nations realized these troubled countries couldn't service their debt and grow at the same time. The US government finally relented and agreed debt relief was a necessary condition for the region's recovery.

In 1989, the new US Treasury secretary, Nicholas Brady, announced the Brady Plan. It was a "voluntary" program that included various options for debt relief and restructuring, depending on the needs of a particular country, including swaps, debt exchanges, debt buybacks, and, most importantly, debt forgiveness.

Each country followed a slightly different path, but Mexico provided the model. Representatives of more than 500 global banks and members of Mexico's government met to negotiate a set of options banks could use to change their exposure to Mexican debt. Three options remained on the table by the end, which became generally known as "Brady Bonds":

1. Swap existing loans for "debt-reduction" bonds, with a 35 percent discount from face value that paid essentially a percentage point above LIBOR.
2. Swap existing loans for 30-year par bonds but with a below-market interest rate of 6.25 percent.
3. Take on new loans at market rates over a four-year period of up to 25 percent of their 1989 exposure.

Nearly half the banks agreed to swap their loans for the discount bonds, while 41 percent chose par bonds and 10 percent gave new money. For forgiving part of Mexico's debt, the banks were given something in return—the backing of the US government.[23] The principal and interest of each bond were securitized by US Treasury bonds, meaning they would receive the full value of their investment in the chance the developing nation defaulted again before the debt term ended (this of course assumed the US would stay solvent, a very likely scenario).

By 1994, 18 countries saw $60 billion of debt forgiven under the Brady Plan, representing nearly $200 billion in bank claims. Most deals forgave about 30 to 35 percent of a country's debt.[24] This debt forgiveness, along with the implicit default protection by the US government, proved largely successful in the ensuing years. With the debt burden reduced, more money flowed through the Latin American economy, stimulating consumption and investment.

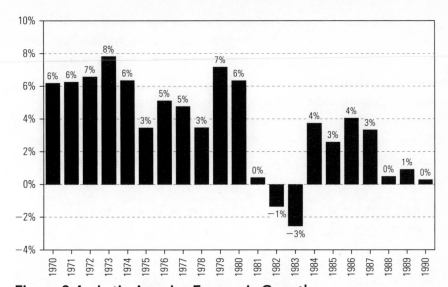

Figure 3.4   Latin America Economic Growth

Source: The World Bank Group; based on the Latin America & Caribbean group as designated by the World Bank.

Economic Ramifications

Not surprisingly, the 1982 debt crisis had dire economic consequences for Latin America. As a whole, the region fell into recession, as illustrated by Figure 3.4. Individual countries were hit harder still—Peru's economy contracted by a whopping 9 percent in 1983.[25]

Latin America rebounded shortly thereafter, but it was a dead cat bounce. Massive debt levels remained, and the economy soon turned downward again. Populist-oriented governments found the prescribed therapy difficult—spending cuts were just too bitter a pill to swallow. Argentina, for example, saw its deficit swell from an already large 15 percent of gross domestic product in 1980 to 1984 to 24 percent in 1985. While the extra government spending provided a boost in the short term, it crowded out vital private investment. Argentina's investment plummeted from an average 22 percent of GDP in the 1970s to 13 percent during the crisis.[26]

Contrast Latin America's recovery to Asia's following its financial crisis discussed in Chapter 2. While Latin America toiled in the economic mud for nearly a decade, Asian economies were quick to rebound—East Asia grew 6 percent in 1999, two years after its crisis, and averaged nearly 9 percent growth in the eight years through 2007.[27] Why were the recoveries so different? The key distinction is political. Asian policymakers quickly swallowed the necessary medicine. But populism left Latin American governments unable to resist the demands of highly mobilized social interests. Latin America's long history of boom-and-bust cycles can be partly attributed to its choice in political models.

Brazil: A Brief Illustration of Populism Following the 1982 Debt Crisis

When the misery of 1982 arrived, Brazil's military government understood the need for a new government built on widespread consensus. The country's industrial-led economic growth "miracle"—from 1968 to 1974 the economy grew at an average yearly rate between 10 and 11 percent—had given way to hyperinflation and labor unrest.[28] And the debt crisis brought the country perilously close to insolvency. Free elections were held at the municipal, state, and federal levels, and the government-approved party won a majority in the electoral college, which was due to vote for a new president in 1985. But the government-approved party was unable to build a consensus, and the opposition party, led by Tancredo Neves, unexpectedly won the presidency.

The masses rejoiced. Neves was a popular figure because he symbolized an end to military rule. From Sao Paulo to Rio de Janeiro, overjoyed citizens showered paper from office windows, blared their car horns, and set off firecrackers. In towns and villages across the country, Brazilians celebrated, literally dancing in the streets.[29] Sadly, Neves was unable to consummate his victory. He passed away before inauguration, leaving the mantle to his vice president, José Sarney.

Sensitive to Neves's popular support and the transitional symbolism behind his rise to power, Sarney began his administration with a keen eye toward appeasing the masses. Not surprisingly, the economy was the biggest concern at the time. Inflation remained stubbornly high from the previous period of industrialization, and the debt crisis had left people agitated about the future. Sarney refused support from the IMF—a popular decision given prevailing nationalist sentiment. He instead announced his own proposal for economic resuscitation, the Cruzado Plan, in 1986. The plan was wide in scope and included price freezes and wage increases between 15 and 34 percent. These policies were very popular—who wouldn't like more money to spend on cheaper goods? A massive consumer boom ensued, and Sarney's popularity surged along with it—opinion polls put his approval rating around 80 percent.[30]

But like virtually every populist government before him, Sarney had difficulty reconciling his social welfare promises with the need for capital. The Brazilian economy was brittle, still struggling under a huge debt burden. Despite a recovery in exports, debt repayments still consumed about a quarter of export earnings.[31] Sarney couldn't acquire more debt under such circumstances. Slashing spending, however, meant cutting the social programs underpinning his popularity—anathema to a populist. Sarney thus chose the only recourse politically available to him: monetary expansion and additional deficit spending.

The Cruzado Plan achieved its political objective. In November 1986, Sarney's party won landslide victories at federal and state elections. However, the deficit financing underpinning the plan sent inflation even higher. Brazil has a long history of high inflation, but Sarney's monetary expansion propelled it to unimaginable heights. Inflation leapt to 629 percent in 1988 and to a remarkable 2,948 percent in 1990 (see Figure 3.5). This meant prices doubled roughly every month!

Sarney tried in vain to enforce wage and price freezes to stop inflation's rampant rise. But the powerful trade unions and industrialists would have nothing of the sort—Sarney had conceded too much to win their support. In a last-ditch effort to cater to the masses, Sarney attempted to redistribute land to help the 10 million landless peasants.[32] Such action met with violent backlash by the large landowners and forced the government to retreat.

Toward the end of the 1980s, the masses began revolting. Riots over escalating food prices and widespread strikes were common.

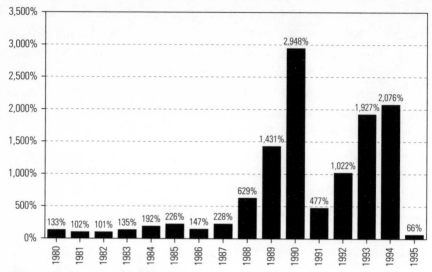

Figure 3.5   Brazil Inflation

Source: International Monetary Fund.

Sarney's political capital all but evaporated, and his party lost crucial positions at municipal elections in 1988. In 1989, he lost his hold on the presidency. The economy plummeted into recession, contracting 4 percent in 1990.[33]

It's probably not too shocking that Brazil's stock market performance over this time was similarly turbulent. To manage hyperinflation, the Brazilian government repeatedly devalued its currency. On February 28, 1986, the Brazilian cruzado replaced the cruzeiro at a rate of 1,000 to 1; on January 15, 1989, the new cruzado replaced the original at the rate of 1,000 to 1. Several other devaluations occurred in the ensuing years and each effectively wiped out the value of the stock market, which fell by 99.99 percent in 1986 and 72 percent in 1990.[34]

Brazil's newly elected president, Fernando Collor de Mello, helped ease inflation by doing the politically unpopular: He cut spending, privatized state companies, and dramatically cut public employment. This was the necessary medicine Sarney's populist administration was politically unwilling to provide. But it was only temporary. Collor de Mello resigned in 1992 due to allegations of corruption, and hyperinflation returned. Ironically, it seemed Brazil's economic progress was at odds with social order.

In retrospect, Sarney's administration followed a fairly predictable pattern common in populist regimes. A charismatic politician wins the favor of the people with promises of economic betterment and wealth redistribution. His popularity soars as his deficit spending-fueled policies spur a brief period of expansion. Soon, rising deficits and inflation get out of hand, erasing gains for the poor. The administration tries a few last-ditch efforts at austerity, but its days are largely numbered. This cycle is repeated ad nauseam through Latin America's history, to negative effect.

THE TEQUILA CRISIS

By the start of the 1990s, it seemed Latin America had learned lessons from the previous crises. Governments pursued austerity measures in earnest and were rewarded with the first signs of economic stabilization in some time. Recovery was slow, but it appeared to finally arrive.

In no other place was this truer than in Mexico, the pariah of the 1982 debt crisis. The economy was liberalized, deregulated, and privatized—a "triple-merit" scenario of free market reform. In an amazing turn of events, Mexico became the darling of foreign investors, and money flocked in faster than it fled nearly 10 years earlier. Prospects seemed limitless. The North American Free Trade Agreement (NAFTA), signed in 1994, confirmed Mexico's rise toward the ranks of the developed world.

Alas, leaving the past behind proved more difficult than expected. The devaluation of the Mexican peso in December 1994 soon turned the boom into another bust. The events were eerily familiar: capital fled, currencies plummeted, inflation skyrocketed, and the banking system neared collapse. What happened?

The Seeds of Recovery

In the years following the 1982 debt crisis, a new political class achieved an increasingly influential voice in Mexico. Politics had long been dominated by the "old guard" within one party—the *Partido Revolucionario Institucional* (PRI)—and a patronage system that stifled anything but the status quo. This new class challenged that existing order. They were educated at top US universities, spoke fluent English, and firmly believed stability came from liberal economics and its tenets: low inflation, stable budgets, deregulated markets, and free trade.[35] In 1985, President Miguel de la Madrid used these principles to lay the seeds of recovery, and his successor, Carlos Salinas, germinated them.

Liberalism

Let's play word association. When you hear the word *liberalism* what immediately comes to mind? Perhaps "left wing" or "Democratic Party"? Most people think of a "liberal" as one who believes that government and interventionist economies (e.g., income redistribution, support of organized labor, etc.) are crucial to protecting individual civil liberties or freedoms. But the true meaning of liberalism is actually the exact opposite of this popular conception. In the classical sense, *liberalism* stands for a limited government, equality of opportunity, and free markets. Rather than "liberal," a more applicable association is *laissez faire*, or literally "allow to do."

De la Madrid correctly saw the vicious cycle of hyperinflation as his administration's most pressing problem. Inflation had taken on a life of its own. Price increases in goods quickly translated to higher wage demands by workers, which in turn led to even higher prices for goods. Inflation averaged nearly 90 percent a year through the debt crisis, hitting a high of 132 percent in 1987. De la Madrid recognized this negative feedback loop needed a new remedy. His program for economic renewal stressed cooperation and coordination in wage and price setting. And it worked—inflation fell to 20 percent by 1990.[36]

Addressing the broader economy, de la Madrid believed in tearing down trade barriers and opening Mexico to the rest of the world. In 1986, he brought Mexico into the General Agreement on Tariffs and Trade (GATT), the predecessor to the World Trade Organization (WTO). Salinas continued the trend, slashing tariffs and signing free trade agreements with many of its Latin American neighbors. Salinas also began negotiations that would lead to NAFTA in 1994.

De la Madrid and Salinas also embarked on the largest deregulation and privatization in Mexican history. More than 3,000 sectors were deregulated, including foreign investment, trucking and bus transportation, and, most importantly, the financial system (which was nationalized in 1982 in a last-ditch attempt to shore up support following default).[37] The scale of change in the mid- to late 1980s was remarkable: Interest rate controls were eliminated, restrictions on the convertibility of the peso removed, and requirements mandating lending to favored sectors abolished. The amount a bank must set aside as collateral with the central bank for a given level of deposits—the reserve requirement ratio—was also drastically cut, freeing funds to find more productive hands.

Exchange Rate Convertibility

When traveling, most take for granted how easy it is to exchange our home currency into our destination's currency. There's a kiosk right at the airport! But in the much larger scale of business and economies, such exchange isn't always so simple. Some countries pass laws restricting the exchange of their currencies or require permits to exchange more than a certain amount. *Convertibility* refers to the degree to which a currency can be freely exchanged, and it varies widely across the world. For example, the US dollar is widely known as a fully convertible currency, meaning there are few, if any, restrictions on its exchange. By contrast, the Indian rupee has numerous restrictions and is generally considered not fully convertible.

Still, it wasn't until the Brady Plan removed the last major impediment to recovery in 1989—Mexico's large debt burden—that the previous year's reforms gained traction. The plan's success opened up the floodgates of economic liberalization.

Distillation

The overall debt relief from the Brady Plan was relatively modest, but it marked a psychological turning point for Mexico. The debt problem receded from domestic political debate, and the plan imbued new confidence, leading to substantially lower interest rates. Within a year, the private sector again sprung to life. It devoured the foreign goods that came with trade liberalization, and banks capitalized on deregulation to expand lending, fueling further consumption and investment. Mexico's current account, which moved to surplus following its default, quickly swung back to deficit. As discussed in Chapter 2, a current account deficit must be matched by a corresponding capital account surplus, meaning Mexico needed additional funds to maintain the increased consumption. Fortunately, Mexico's reforms were not unnoticed by foreign investors.

Around this time, the structure of global capital markets began to change. The days when foreign bank loans dominated financing for emerging markets were passing, as portfolio flows played an increasingly important role—investment managers across the world were discovering exciting new opportunities in emerging markets. In Mexico's case, another key event spurred interest in its markets: US interest rates declined at the beginning of the 1990s as the Federal Reserve fought off recession. With confidence in Mexico already rising, it offered an easy alternative to its yield-deprived neighbors to the North.

Money flowed in, creating a virtuous cycle: Capital inflows led to further increases in bank lending, which further stimulated investment and consumption. In 1993 alone, over $30 billion in foreign capital was invested.[38] Fattened by the inflows, Mexico's banks became international leaders. In 1992, three of the 25 most profitable banks in the world were domiciled in Mexico. By 1993, that number was seven.[39] Equity markets were also red-hot. In the six years ending in 1993, the stock market rose 61 percent on average *each year*. In 1991 alone, the Mexican market leapt 121 percent![40] The media began talking of a "new" Latin America and the "Mexican miracle."[41]

But warning signs were brewing on the horizon. Mexico's currency, the peso, was restricted to a band against the US dollar in 1991, with the lower end of the band set to decline by a small amount each day to allow for gradual depreciation. Yet the scale of inflows meant the actual rate continuously hit the high end. In time, many observers began loudly worrying the peso was overvalued.

There were also signs banks were becoming lax in their lending. Despite all the reform, structural inefficiencies remained in the banking system. For example, there was no central credit bureau to help lenders evaluate a borrower's creditworthiness. Regulatory oversight was minimal. By the end of 1993, however, such concerns were of no consequence to Mexican authorities, as they continued to encourage bank lending and consumption.

Meanwhile, two key events seemed to cement Mexico's ascension to the world stage. On New Year's Day 1994, the North American Free Trade Agreement (NAFTA) took effect. Mexico's growing industry now had unencumbered access to the world's biggest market—the US. In March of the same year, it entered the Organisation for Economic Cooperation and Development (OECD), the world's pre-eminent club of rich countries.

But militants in Mexico's Chiapas region had different ideas. The reform years left the country's poor agrarian workers struggling beneath the veneer of economic revival. Mexico's technocrats and elites benefited from the newfound interconnectedness to the global economy, but rural residents remained destitute and increasingly disenfranchised. Chiapas was one of Mexico's poorest rural regions, and its residents reacted violently to the signing of the agreement. The outbreak was quickly quelled by the government but served as a brutal reminder of Mexico's problems.

A few months later, Luis Colosio, Carlos Salinas' hand-picked successor, was assassinated on the campaign trail. With the Chiapas uprising still fresh in investors' minds, additional political turmoil was too frightening a prospect. Foreign capital inflows quickly dried up and began to reverse. Mexico's rise was quickly jeopardized by two unexpected exogenous shocks.

The Ensuing Hangover

Faced with a massive exodus of capital, Mexican authorities needed to react quickly. Officials could raise short-term interest rates to entice investors to keep their cash in pesos. But this rise in interest rates would hurt consumers and businesses, not to mention exacerbate the non-performing loans accumulated on bank balance sheets. They could reintroduce restrictions on the convertibility of the peso, essentially prohibiting foreign investors from exchanging the currency. But that would call into question the country's adherence to economic liberalism, a key driver behind the recent boom. Or they could devalue the peso, which was fixed to a band since 1991.

Authorities chose the latter, but it took time before they completely acquiesced. In the months following Colosio's assassination, the government used foreign exchange reserves built up during the years of inflows to offset outflows. But these reserves were not large enough to avert crisis for long. Rather than admit defeat and devalue, the government began issuing *tesobonos*—short-term government bonds indexed to US dollars—to supplement reserves. Officials used these borrowed funds as part of its peso defense. This strategy left Mexico increasingly vulnerable to a liquidity crisis; the government needed to roll over this short-term debt every few months in addition to satisfying its other foreign creditors.[42]

The confidence inspired by the Brady Plan was evaporating, and interest rates on one-month Treasury bills more than doubled in December 1994 to 31 percent.[43] The pressure was soon too much. Mexico finally caved on December 20 and devalued the peso by widening its trading band by approximately 15 percent (see Figure 3.6). But the devaluation wasn't large enough to appease speculators. The market immediately began pricing in a second round. Just two days later, authorities were forced to freely float the peso.[44] It immediately sunk like a stone.

The most immediate problem was the deterioration of Mexico's fiscal position. Mexico issued billions of tesobonos during its currency defense, leaving it acutely exposed to moves in the peso/US dollar exchange rate. With the peso plummeting, the value of this debt soared. To make matters worse, as the news of the tesobono problem spread, panic set in, and investors rushed to sell their bonds—yet another vicious cycle.

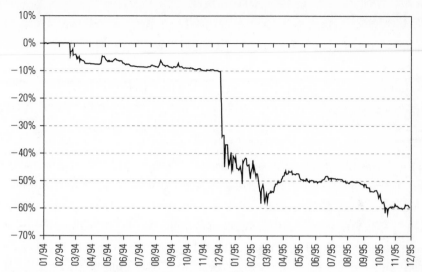

Figure 3.6   Mexican Peso vs. US Dollar
Source: Thomson Datastream.

By now, you should know what's coming next: Mexico's economy collapsed, and the "Tequila Crisis" was born. Economic growth contracted by 6 percent in 1995—nearly double the fall following the 1982 debt crisis. The local stock exchange, the *Bolsa Mexicana de Valores* (BMV), also crashed, falling 44 percent in 1994 and 23 percent in 1995. It would be nearly 10 years before the BMV returned to the same level. As in previous crises, Mexico's implosion soon infected other Latin American countries, despite no fundamental connections. Argentina was particularly hard hit. Speculators attacked its currency, and its financial system nearly collapsed.

With few financial resources of its own, Latin America turned to the outside world for help. And again the Western world obliged; the US Treasury extended a $50 billion line of credit to Mexico, and Argentina received $12 billion from the World Bank. But unlike the several years of slow healing following the 1980s debt fiasco, Mexico made a remarkably swift recovery. In a few years time, the next boom had begun.

Implications

The Tequila Crisis is yet another reminder to investors that economic success and media admiration don't make a country immune to crisis. While the Mexican government made clear policy errors, including ignoring an overvalued exchange rate and letting credit spiral, there are several broader implications important to investors.

The Four Most Dangerous Words   During Mexico's early 1990s boom, the media couldn't help itself, issuing proclamations of a "new" era. No more boom and bust! It certainly seemed possible at the time. Everything *was* going amazingly well. But famous investor John Templeton's legendary phrase is perhaps most fitting: The world's four most dangerous investing words are "It's different this time." It never is. It always just *feels* that way. If you hear the media shout these words, it's wise to turn a deaf ear.

Contagion   As with the Asian Financial Crisis in the late 1990s, contagion struck Latin America following Mexico's crisis. Contagion is ultimately rooted in fear or, said another way, a pervasive lack of confidence. Here's an example of how it works: Suppose you were the loan officer in a big Wall Street bank in 1982. You were fortunate enough not to have exposure to Mexican debt, but the trouble there led you to reevaluate your exposure to the loans you made to a few Argentine businesses over the years. You decide not to renew some of their loans and ask for repayment. To repay the loan, the Argentine businesses must acquire pesos, which will most likely come from the local bank. The local Argentine bank will in turn have to recall some of its loans to meet the withdrawals, leading to a further reduction in credit. As more and more credit gets called in, businesses begin having trouble repaying on such short notice. Depositors begin to wonder if the banks can fully collect from their clients and begin to withdraw money, just in case. The panic feeds on itself—a negative feedback loop begins that decimates markets and the real economy. While the exact order of events varies by country and crisis, the sentiment behind each is the same.[45]

Credit Crisis, Emerging Markets Style   No matter the cause, credit or banking crises tend to elicit a similar reaction—panic. In most cases, the fear is temporal—that one's money will disappear into the abyss if not retrieved fast enough. Crises in emerging markets follow a similar logic but with one slight difference: Investors are not only concerned with recovering their assets, but also with losing *purchasing power*. Every major emerging market crisis involved a substantial decline in the country's currency as well. In some cases, the currency is the catalyst. In others, it's another asset sold off in the ensuing panic. Whatever the cause, the currency decline is a double whammy to investors, since the *real* value of their investment falls in addition to the *nominal* value.

The Importance of Politics in Emerging Markets   Last, Mexico's experience with the Tequila Crisis reveals how quickly the political environment can impact markets, particularly in volatile emerging markets. Investors were wildly optimistic about Mexico's liberal market reforms and economic prospects. But it is the unexpected that moves markets. The revolt in Chiapas and assassination of Luis Colosio quickly overwhelmed any prior positive developments, sending markets into a tailspin. While it's difficult to predict these types of events, investors should always include an analysis of the political environment in any investment decision (more on this in Chapter 6).

Chapter Recap

Latin America's recent capital markets history reflects its reputation as the most troubled of emerging market regions.

- Its flirtation with populism encouraged reckless fiscal and monetary policy as governments struggled to reconcile social welfare promises with the need for capital, often to devastating effect.
  - Populist policies exacerbated the volatility of Latin American capital markets, promoting hyperinflation, excess debt levels, and wealth redistribution. The events surrounding the 1982 debt crisis illustrate these struggles.
- Mexico in the 1990s reminded investors of the four most dangerous words: "It's different this time."
  - Media adoration and positive reforms masked the country's over-reliance on foreign debt—a common theme throughout Latin America's history.
- With nearly continuous cycles of boom and bust, it's easy for investors to casually dismiss the region and eschew the volatility.
- But the region's vast resources and economic potential warrant consideration. To successfully invest in Latin America, however, investors must remain cognizant of its cyclical past.

4

FROM THE RUBBLE OF THE IRON CURTAIN TO THE LEGACY OF APARTHEID

In 1991, the ideological struggle enveloping the world for nearly a half century ended after the Soviet Union collapsed under its own weight. The turmoil that followed Russia's transition to capitalism and democracy left no corner of society untouched. A select few, the "oligarchs," capitalized from the chaotic times, acquiring untold wealth and power through political connections. Yet most Russians remained destitute and disenchanted, yearning for the powerful leaders of yesteryear.

After crisis hit again in 1998, Russians would soon get their wish—Vladimir Putin brought Russia nearly full circle with the ideologies of its Soviet past. His was a unique form of state-led, oily capitalism, and the ensuing recentralization of key energy and materials assets under his rule would alter the investment landscape. The Soviet Union's collapse and the ensuing years of reform reveal the effects of unbridled, state-concentrated political power on markets.

We'll first examine Russia, then shift south to dissect South Africa's turbulent legacy of racial relations and markets. Apartheid, a system of legal racial segregation with the minority as the dominant force, blighted one of Africa's most prosperous and promising nations. It is an unfortunate page in history, but it offers unique lessons for investors.

THE RUBBLE OF THE IRON CURTAIN

Mikhail Gorbachev came to power as the Communist Party's general Secretary in 1985 (the de-facto head of state for the Soviet Union), following a brief period of musical chairs at the end of Leonid Brezhnev's 20-year regime. Gorbachev represented a new vein of Soviet thinkers. He was the first Communist leader born after the Bolshevik Revolution, and grew up in a generation exposed to a range of intellectual freedoms denied under previous regimes. He was well-educated—with a law degree from the prestigious Moscow University and an advanced economics degree—and worldly, with exposure to a wide swath of intellectual thought. He symbolized a break from the country's technocratic and anti-intellectual predecessors.

Despite the problems and hardships endured because of the Soviet system, Gorbachev's generation still firmly believed it could be reformed. To them, the Soviet Union held a unique place in the world—not in isolation from the West but right alongside it.[1] Gorbachev's ambition was to bring the Soviet Union closer to the modern world.

Conscious of the weight of history, Gorbachev knew he must build political support to have any chance of breaking the state away from anachronistic Soviet norms. After all, nowhere else in the world did the state penetrate as deeply into society. It intruded everywhere, and almost everyone was connected to it in some form. Many staked their livelihoods on its continuation and gained self-worth from their rank within it. Given the corruption, embedded self-interests, and rampant poverty throughout the Soviet system, adherence to its ideals seemed paradoxical. But the power of the Soviet empire was a profound source of pride to many of its citizens, inextricably intertwined with their identity.

Gorbachev stumbled out of the gate. In early 1986, an experiment at the Chernobyl nuclear power plant in northern Ukraine went horribly awry, sending a plume of radiation nearly a mile into the sky.[2] Gorbachev took 18 days to disclose the accident to the world—an eternity given the gravity of events. The resulting social and political fallout was enormous. The Communist Party spent over half a century carefully crafting its image of a state in complete control, and Chernobyl suddenly threw this into question.

Glasnost and Perestroika

Losing support by the day, Gorbachev sped up his reform agenda, embarking on a flurry of activity. His overarching philosophy rested on two concepts: *glasnost* (reform, openness, and transparency) and *perestroika* (restructuring). In the next few years, he opened the media (which had served as mouthpiece of the state for decades), signed a joint venture law to attract foreign capital, and issued several other similar decrees. More subtly, he empowered Soviet businesses and citizens to do anything not explicitly forbidden; whereas, in the past, they adhered to a list of permitted activities.

But glasnost and perestroika had the unintended consequence of further revealing the ugliness behind the powerful Soviet façade. It was soon evident to the world just how brittle, secretive, and insecure the country was after 70 years of isolation. It may have looked like a superpower from the outside—and in many ways it was—but beneath the exterior it largely remained a third-world country.

Life was a struggle for most Russians—they often lacked the simplest necessities, from matches to toothpaste to hosiery. Gorbachev's policies of transparency also revealed something much larger and more subversive—the illegitimacy and hypocrisy of the state. The Communist Party ruled with an iron fist, poisoning society with an incestuous mix of economic and political power. Despite his best intentions, Gorbachev unintentionally exposed the grim realities of the Soviet system.

Gorbachev's reforms didn't resonate with the populace as much as he hoped. In hindsight, this was understandable. Decades of totalitarian and centrally planned rule had left the population unable to interpret market-based reforms in the proper context. In fact the word "market" itself was prohibited in the Soviet Union.[3] Moreover, few even knew how to capitalize (pardon the pun) on such a system. Those who did were connected politically to previous regimes and had much to lose from a declining state. It simply proved too difficult to quickly reverse such an embedded worldview.

Politically, Gorbachev was stuck in a more complicated position than his predecessors. He increasingly found himself caught between two distinct groups within the Communist Party: the conservatives, who wanted to stop reform, and the liberals, led by the enigmatic Boris Yeltsin, who wanted to accelerate it. These two sides were moving further and further apart in the late 1980s. In response to pressure from Yeltsin to speed the pace of reform, Gorbachev created the Congress of People's Deputies (CPD) in 1988—a legislature with two-thirds of its deputies chosen through uncontested elections.

Such a move was unfathomable in the Soviet heyday—the very fabric of the Soviet state rested on the Communist Party's leading role. The CPD ushered in the first legal opposition in nearly 60 years at the 1989 parliamentary elections, though it was only a small minority.[4] Gorbachev's consensus-building created a multiparty system at odds with the existing structure of government.[5] He didn't realize it at the time, but the move was a major tipping point toward the Soviet Union's collapse.

Gorbachev's reforms also exposed deep-rooted but hidden issues of nationality and identity in the Soviet satellite states. In August 1989, a non-communist government was elected in Poland. The Berlin Wall—a highly symbolic barrier of the Iron Curtain—crumbled in November 1989. And in March 1990, Lithuania declared its independence. Turning one's back on the Soviet Union was intolerable, even to Gorbachev. He responded forcefully. In Lithuania, for example, Gorbachev sent in the KGB and imposed economic sanctions, revealing the bluntness of Soviet power.

But those efforts failed. By the start of the 1990s, Gorbachev's legitimacy hung by a thread. Boris Yeltsin and the liberal opposition were increasingly vocal. In March 1990, radical democrats won control of the largest and most populous of the country's republics—the Russian Soviet Federative Socialist Republic. The group declared sovereignty for Russia, as the territory would be named, and Yeltsin was soon named its leader.

Gorbachev tried several desperate attempts to cling to power, but they proved unsuccessful. An ill-fated coup d'état in August 1991, organized by the entire Gorbachev team (except Gorbachev himself, who was mysteriously on vacation), proved to be the old regime's last gasp. Yeltsin easily squashed the coup, and the Soviet Union collapsed with Gorbachev's resignation on December 25, 1991.

THE WILD, WILD EAST

Yeltsin swiftly set about dismantling the Soviet system. The enormity of this change cannot be understated. Virtually overnight, an entirely new system was built from the crumbling remnants of the old: A command economy was now a market system, and an authoritarian socialist state was now a democracy. Not surprisingly, the transition was tumultuous, and the turmoil would dominate the next decade—its effects rippling across the globe.

The first few years of Yeltsin's administration were a veritable no-man's land, stuck between two systems inherently at odds with each other. A major problem was quickly apparent—in the early stages, no one knew what they were doing, at least not beyond the most basic theoretical level. Yeltsin may have staked his political career on the dismantling of communism and centrally planned economics, but, just like his predecessors, he too was a product of the Soviet era. He had no experience with making a market system work. As such, he first focused on action for the sake of action—rules and institutions could wait.

This translated into his "shock therapy" program, which included immediate price deregulation, higher taxes, the lowering of import barriers, increased trade with the rest of the world, and huge cuts to government spending. Many of these initiatives were appropriately based in free market principles, but the precarious environment at the time gave little chance for success.

Privatization

The privatization of state-run enterprises was a crucial requirement for the transition to a market economy. In the Soviet Union, there was no distinction between a company and the state—they were one and the same. Gorbachev brought forth the idea of privatization, but it wasn't until after the collapse of the Soviet Union that it was possible. Interestingly, the privatization scheme announced in 1992 marked the formative years of Russia's first stock exchange (officially established in 1995).

The program relied heavily on voucher-based privatization. The value of state ownership, estimated at 1.5 trillion rubles, was distributed equally among the 146 million citizens. Every Russian received a voucher for 10,000 rubles, with the right to do essentially whatever they wished. Most exchanged the voucher for shares in their employing company, participated in auctions for shares of others, bought shares of an intermediary organization (or investment fund), or simply sold the voucher for cash.[6]

The latter soon became a widespread business, and enterprising individuals set up shop to entice people with the draw of immediate hard cash. These resellers in turn exchanged vouchers for shares in privatized companies or sold them again at stock exchanges. The first voucher trades occurred on the Russian raw materials stock exchange (RTSE) on October 1, 1992. Soon the voucher paper became the most actively traded issue on the exchange. In 1993, voucher transaction volume on the RTSE accounted for 75 percent of total turnover.[7] Russia's earliest shareholders acquired stakes in companies in this manner. In the end, over 46,000 companies were privatized in 1992. By 1995, the number reached 122,000, or more than half of Russia's total enterprises.[8]

But the voucher program had exposed a recurring flaw in Russia's transition to capitalism—the lack of capital markets infrastructure. Without solid institutions underlying markets, capitalism exists in name only. Thousands of investment funds appeared overnight, offering outrageously high returns. The vast majority were scams and Ponzi schemes. The most famous was the MMM fund, which advertised on television (a novelty considering the media was now free from Communist control), promising returns upwards of 3,000 percent. It was too tempting for many to resist. In mid-1993, shares of MMM sold for 10,000 rubles. A year later, they sold for more than 100,000. After the fund's collapse in 1994, it was estimated 300 million shares were outstanding and over 10 million people were swindled.[9] Others suffered similar fates at similar funds.

Descending Into Chaos

The ramifications of Yeltsin's economic reforms were immediately apparent. The fall of the Soviet Union was more economically devastating than any other event in modern history, arguably by several orders of magnitude. Even before the Soviet Union's collapse, the economy was dangerously close to a precipice. But Yeltsin's transition sent it into freefall. Shortages, rationing, and queues for basic goods became common. Abolishment of state subsidies resulted in hyperinflation, with prices rising over 2,600 percent in 1992 alone.[10] Productive members of the Soviet state found themselves powerless in the new system, adding to a sense of despair. In 1993, the economy contracted 9 percent. It fell another 13 percent in 1994 and 4 percent in both 1995 and 1996. Figures are not available for 1992, but they were likely even worse.[11] In the span of six years, the economy contracted by at least a third.

Meanwhile, the political scene also descended into chaos. Yeltsin's motives behind his "shock therapy" program were probably more political than economic. More than anything else, he feared Communists returning to power. Thus, many of his actions were predicated on removing as much power from the government's hands as possible. The ensuing decentralization left control of the various states at the hands of the respective regions, adding to the sense no one was manning the ship.

By 1993, tensions between Yeltsin and other members of Parliament reached a fever pitch. Yeltsin, fed up with the legislature slowing down his reforms, dissolved Parliament and called elections. His opposition barricaded itself in Parliament, a makeshift attempt at a coup d'état. But with a little bit of violence, Yeltsin easily squashed the revolt. He pushed through a new constitution giving him supreme, "super" presidential powers. In effect, his powers were no less absolute than the Soviet Union's General Party Secretary. Over the next few years, Yeltsin issued thousands of decrees, or presidentially mandated laws. Pure Russian democracy proved short-lived.

Parliamentary System

The most widespread system of government around the world is the *parliamentary system*. There are variations of the model, but it generally includes a clear delineation between the head of government and the head of state. The head of government is usually the *prime minister* or *premier*. The *prime minister* heads the legislature, often split into two houses—a lower and upper—to create checks and balances. The head of state is either the *president* (elected either by popular vote or by parliament itself) or a hereditary *monarch*. Heads of state are generally ceremonial, but in some cases (like in Russia), they can be quite powerful. In either case, the head of state holds the ultimate trump card—the ability to dissolve the government and call elections.

To maintain power, Yeltsin had to forgo a substantial amount of political capital. By 1996, Russians had given him several second chances for his reforms to bear fruit, but most still lived in impoverished and miserable conditions. Elections were scheduled for the end of the year, and Yeltsin's support was remarkably low—his approval rating a mere 8 percent. Even worse, the Communist Party's candidate had 24 percent of voters' support.[12]

Loans-for-Shares and the Rise of the Oligarchs

As elections approached in 1996, the economic situation was perilous— the government was bankrupt. In late 1995, Vladimir Potanin, head of the powerful bank Oneximbank, offered the government a solution to its money problem. The State Duma, the lower house of Parliament, had blocked privatizations of state energy and materials enterprises because of their national importance. Potanin proposed commercial banks offer loans to the government, collateralized by shares in these companies. This unleashed a second wave of privatization. The "loans-for-shares" scheme, as it would be called, was a seminal event in post-Soviet history.

The government auctioned controlling stakes in companies on a competitive basis to banks in exchange for loans. But there was a catch. Everyone knew the loans wouldn't really be loans—the bankers held no hope the government would repay them given the precarious state of affairs. In effect, the bankers were trading cash for the ability to purchase strategic state assets. Still, it was a mutually beneficial situation. The state wouldn't starve, and the banks received the right to acquire valuable, previously unattainable assets in return.

On paper, the arrangement was perfectly legitimate. Theoretically, interested parties competed for shares, meaning the assets would be sold for whatever the market deemed appropriate. Unfortunately, the actual mechanics turned out to be nowhere close to such an ideal—a remarkable trail of corruption, vested interests, and downright theft followed.

The auctions began inauspiciously. Scheduled to begin promptly with the New Year, there were only a short few months to establish logistics. Potanin shrewdly leveraged this short time frame to get partial control over the process. Oneximbank and several other financial institutions close to the government (Menatep, SBS-Agro) convinced Yeltsin they were best suited to run the auctions—a blatant conflict of interest.

Once the auctions kicked off in earnest in 1996, the real fun began. The law required at least two bidders for a valid auction, but corruption was rampant. Often, the winner was agreed upon beforehand, and the second bidder was a fake corporation. For example, in the auction for shares of Novolipetsk Steel (NLMK), one of the world's largest steel producers, Oneximbank essentially competed against itself through a subsidiary to provide the illusion of a fair sale.

Even more egregious were the bid amounts. The government was in a bind and desperate for funds, meaning it would be forced to sell the assets at somewhat depressed prices. But the actual terms were beyond imagination. Consider the following:

- Oneximbank gave the government $170 million for a 51 percent voting share of Norilsk Nickel, which produces 90 percent of Russia's nickel and cobalt and 100 percent of its platinum. A Western insurance company covered it for $30 billion shortly thereafter, over 100 times more than the purchase price.[13]
- The energy giant Gazprom sold for $250 million. Gazprom controls a third of the world's natural gas resources, is the sole gas supplier to the former Soviet Union, and provides Western Europe with about a fifth of its natural gas. If it were a Western energy company, it would have easily been valued 100 times more.[14]
- Potanin loaned the government $130 million for 51 percent of Sidanco, the Russian oil company. Within a year, he sold just 10 percent of the company to British Petroleum for $571 million.[15]
- Mikhail Khodorkovsky, who controlled the bank Menatep, acquired Yukos, Russia's second largest oil company, for $150 million.
- The market value of six of Russia's most important industrial companies—Gazprom, RAO UES, Lukoil, Rostelecom, Yuganskneftegaz, and Surgutneftegaz—mysteriously grew 18 to 26 times their auction price a mere one and a half years later.[16]

By the end of the 1990s, less than 20 Russian companies and banks controlled 70 percent of the economy.[17] The power and wealth of the Soviet empire fell into the laps of a fortunate few. These men represented the new "Russian oligarchy," commonly known as the *oligarchs*.

The oligarchs profoundly altered the course of Russian politics and markets for years to come. They were open to market-based reforms, but not because they were true capitalists. Rather, such reforms provided a shield against the return of a centrally planned economy, which threatened their prominence. The oligarchs influenced all forms of government policy, from economics to legislation, and dipped their hands in the political sphere by sponsoring ministers and members of parliament. They even managed to propel Yeltsin to victory in the 1996 elections despite his failing health and low approval ratings. In short, they used their newly acquired power to receive favorable treatment and ensure their financial interests remained protected from competition.

The oligarch saga also revealed the importance of the Energy and Materials sectors. The Russian economy runs on it. Energy accounts for over 60 percent of Russian exports and approximately 20 percent of total output.[18] If you include the industry and transportation critical to its production and distribution, its contribution to economic output is even higher. You can see why the oligarchs were so motivated to get their hands on such assets.

Their share of the stock market is even more profound—Russia's Energy and Materials sectors account for three-quarters of its total market capitalization.[19] Therefore, changes in oil prices have a tremendous impact on the overall Russian economy and stock market. Though historical data are limited, Figure 4.1 shows the directional relationship between the price of oil and Russian stocks. The lesson for investors: Russia is inescapably tied to commodity prices.

The second wave of privatization also heralded a new set of investors. Western bankers were omnipresent in Russia and deal making

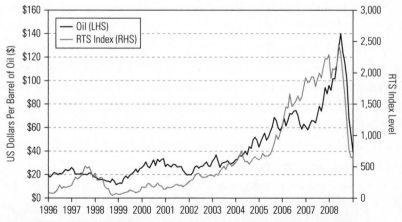

Figure 4.1   Russian Stock Market and the Price of Oil
Source: Global Financial Data.

surged. Many oligarchs used this international buzz to fuel expansion of their newly acquired empires with foreign capital. Alexander Smolensky, the oligarch in charge of the powerful SBS-Agro bank, borrowed $168 million from two Western banks and floated a $250 million Eurobond. He later admitted he didn't know what he would do with the money from the bond issuance, but he went along with it because the lenders said he could.[20] This optimism translated into huge gains for the budding stock market, which returned 98 percent in 1997.[21]

CRISIS STRIKES AGAIN—THE 1998 RUBLE CRISIS

Despite the glossy appearance, Russia fundamentally remained in dire straits. Inflation reduced real wages to half their Soviet levels, and only about 40 percent of workers were paid on time. The oligarchs dramatically reduced their tax payments as payback for securing Yeltsin's election victory—nearly all the main companies with tax arrears at the end of 1996 were energy companies.[22] The price of oil collapsed, depriving the government of another large revenue source. And the government remained chronically undisciplined in its spending.[23] Russia found itself stuck in a fiscal tsunami.

Previously, the government printed money to meet its deficit, but it stopped doing so by the mid-1990s because of hyperinflation's destabilizing effects. Starting in 1993, it began to borrow on the capital markets. The government issued short-term bonds, usually with a three- to six-month term, called GKOs (an abbreviation of the Russian for "short-term government obligations"). The initial amounts were tiny. By year end 1994, only $3 billion were outstanding. But the amount soon exploded—by mid-1998, there were nearly $70 billion in GKOs.[24] To put this in context, Russia's total nominal economic output was around $400 billion.[25]

It was no secret the Russian economy had problems, yet GKOs still managed to attract interest. Every investor has his price, and Russia paid a pretty penny—short-term interest rates were 200 percent at the start of 1995.[26] These high rates had a perverse effect, diverting capital away from more economically productive assets. Foreigners had little desire to invest directly in Russian projects when they could earn several hundred percent in the span of a few months. Few Russian companies did either, for that matter. This meant that desperately needed infrastructure and development projects moved forward ever more slowly.

The government initially used these bonds as intended—to finance the deficit. However, the interest rate payments soon proved too exorbitant. In 1994, 75 percent of the proceeds from GKOs went to cover the deficit. By 1997, 91 percent were used to pay off previously issued bonds, leaving only 9 percent for new spending![27] Not surprisingly, the government soon ran into a shortfall. In April 1998, for the first time, the money collected from new GKO issuance was less than what was needed to pay off investors—the government had to delve into alternative funding sources for another $164 million. The shortfall rose over the next several months and hit $10 billion in early July.

Something more ominous was also brewing on the horizon— the Asian Financial Crisis. As we mentioned in Chapter 2, currency problems in Asia spread swiftly across the globe to seemingly unconnected markets. One of those markets was Russia. In 1995, the government had pegged the ruble to a range versus the dollar to finally tame inflation. Though the peg had the desired effect, the flood of investor capital from GKO bonds and renewed international interest left many believing the ruble was overvalued. Speculators were on the prowl searching for weakened emerging markets, and they soon swooped down on Russia—putting enormous downward pressure on the ruble. The government was forced to spend its currency reserves in defense. It was estimated that, between October 1997 and August 1998, the Russian central bank spent $27 billion of US dollar reserves to keep the peg, on top of a $5 billion loan from the World Bank and IMF.[28]

Finally, on August 13, 1998, Russian markets relented under the conflux of pressures—stock, bond, and currency markets collapsed as Russia ended its increasingly desperate attempts to keep the

Exchange Rates and Inflation

Russia's decision to convert to a fixed exchange system in 1995 effectively brought down inflation. We know currencies are influenced by inflation and vice versa. A high rate of inflation decreases demand for a currency due to the relative loss of purchasing power, leading to depreciation. The opposite also holds true. But how might the exchange rate system itself relate to inflation, specifically a fixed regime? Mostly, it's a confidence game—a currency peg increases the willingness of investors to hold the currency since they are more certain of its value. There are other ancillary effects too, such as the political costs of abandoning the peg, which promotes sounder policies.

Source: Atish R Ghosh, Ann-Marie Gulde, Jonathan D. Ostry, and Holger Wolf, "Does the Exchange Rate Regime Matter for Inflation and Growth," Economic Issues No. 2 (September 1996).

country solvent. Within a month, the ruble fell more than 70 percent (see Figure 4.2). What little savings Russians had became effectively worthless. After falling to a manageable 11 percent in 1997, inflation reignited to 84 percent in 1998. The stock market fell 85 percent.[29] Some of Russia's biggest, most influential companies—and their associated oligarchs—also collapsed.

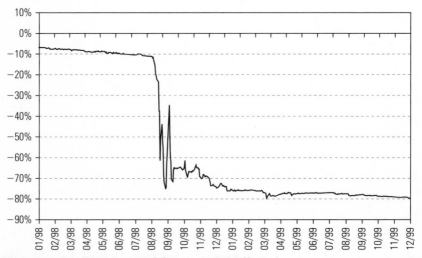

Figure 4.2   Russian Ruble vs. US Dollar
Source: Thomson Datastream.

PUTIN AND THE MODERN SOVIET STATE

An outside observer taking stock of Russia in the wake of the crisis would have been horrified. By 1998, the economy had officially contracted by nearly a third since the fall of the Soviet Union.[30] Unofficially, that number was likely much higher. Institutions were weak and sickly. The government lost all semblance of legitimacy. And the average Russian wallowed in extreme poverty, resenting the farce of the privatization process. Simply put, the past decade was a disaster. The country was ripe for change, and it came from an unexpected source.

Elections were due in 2000, and the oligarchs, who effectively controlled the country, sought a suitable replacement for Boris Yeltsin. They had their eye on a relative unknown, Vladimir Putin, then head of the Federal Security Service (FSB), the successor to the infamous KGB. They saw Putin as someone capable of leading the country but not someone who would seek to unwind the privatization results (and thus their wealth). Not surprisingly, they got their way—Yeltsin named Putin to be prime minister in August 1999, the fifth man to hold that job in the past two years.[31] On New Year's Eve, Yeltsin unexpectedly announced he was passing the duties of president to Putin. The public reaction was mixed, and Putin's 30 percent approval rating was commensurate with his status as a relative newcomer. But Putin's calm and measured responses to guerrilla attacks in late 1999 (presaging the war in Chechnya) led to a surge in his popularity. In mere months, his approval rating soared to 80 percent. It has been strong ever since.

Putin won presidential elections in 2000 with a strong moral mandate, securing 52.5 percent of the popular vote.[32] He perfectly fit the country's cultural identity and thirst for political power. Despite several years of Western, free-market thought, Russian culture remained rooted in a centuries-old obedience to authority, from the great tsars to the Soviet empire. The country's Orthodox Christianity religious heritage also left a strong moral aversion to greed, pride, and excessive wealth. With this in mind, it's not surprising to see how quickly Putin achieved widespread popularity—he symbolized a return to the powerful figures of the past.

To accomplish his goals, Putin needed to renegotiate the state's previously entrenched relationship with the oligarchs. He made clear early on he didn't intend to embark on a renationalization campaign given the chaos and struggle that would ensue. Instead, he offered a bargain: If the oligarchs paid their taxes and stayed out of politics, they could keep the property they acquired under the previous administration.

Meanwhile, the economy showed signs of a remarkably swift recovery from the 1998 crisis. Russian gross domestic product grew a healthy 6 percent in 1999, followed by 10 percent in 2000.[33] The ruble devaluation restored competitiveness to the trade sector, which was previously decimated by cheap imports. Extensive restructuring with the London Club of commercial creditors helped ease the country's massive debt burden.

Many of Putin's first policies as president also aided the recovery. Between 2000 and 2003, he pushed through a flat personal tax at 13 percent, one of the lowest rates in the world, and substantially lowered corporate rates. Lower taxes stimulate investment and consumption by putting more money into productive hands (i.e., the private sector). They also increase the willingness of people to actually pay the taxes. Additionally, Putin updated the labor code, legalized the purchase and sale of both urban and agricultural land, and dramatically reduced bureaucratic red tape.

Perhaps most importantly, however, Putin's firm grip on power gave the country a degree of stability and predictability that were largely absent in the tumultuous 1990s. That grip would soon be tested, with lasting implications for investors. The 2003 Yukos affair signaled a turning point in Putin's laissez-faire relationship with the oligarchs. It also proved to be something much more: Russia reacquainted itself with its Soviet past.

Yukos and the Lessons of History

The oligarch Mikhail Khodorkovsky acquired Yukos, Russia's second-largest energy company, in the loans-for-shares auctions. At the time, Khodorkovsky controlled Menatep, one of the privileged banks coordinating the privatization auctions, and he leveraged this power to purchase 45 percent of Yukos. Menatep disqualified several competing bids on formalities, eventually paying $150 million for the shares. It also agreed to finance $200 million of development projects for the company, which made the total price a very reasonable $350 million.

There was no question Khodorkovsky got a deal. But the figures are more complicated than at first glance. The company was far from profitable and laden with debt—it had a negative net worth of about $3.5 billion.[34] Its *lifting* costs—or the cost to get oil out of the ground—were prohibitively high due to decades of underinvestment. No foreign company wanted anything to do with it.

In 1996, Khodorkovsky left his post at Menatep and joined Yukos management as a vice president. Two months later, he became the chairman of the board. With Khodorkovsky at the helm, the company turned around. He invested heavily in technology and infrastructure, leading to remarkable gains in efficiency over the next few years— Yukos's lifting costs were reduced eight times, to $1.57 per barrel. The company expanded to 50 regions in Russia—a 10-fold increase in the period following the takeover. Production reached 86 million tons of oil per year—double that of 1998. The company's market capitalization increased from $350 million to over $10 billion.[35]

Khodorkovsky also instilled levels of transparency unfathomable to those accustomed to the climate of secrecy underpinning Russian capitalism. In 2002, he publicly disclosed Yukos's ownership structure, and his dealings increasingly adhered to Western standards. Yukos became a well-respected and influential international organization, and Khodorkovsky symbolized a new and improved Russia, based in Western values and flush with opportunities.

Success also reformed Khodorkovsky. He was no longer content to play the role of obedient oligarch and began openly challenging the corrupt business practices dominating Russian society. Putin regularly met with key business leaders, and in a February 20, 2003, meeting, Khodorkovsky openly challenged Putin on rampant government corruption. Specifically, he drew attention to a recent deal where state-owned Rosneft outbid Yukos for a small oil company with an outrageously large sum (the acquired company was run by a friend of

Putin's). In return, Putin questioned Khodorkovsky's own acquisition of Yukos. The day proved highly symbolic—the grand bargain struck between Putin and the oligarchs was breached.

The ensuing events recalled the unchecked political power under Soviet rule. On July 2, 2003, one of Khodorkovsky's lieutenants was arrested on charges of embezzlement. Police raids on Yukos buildings and a government investigation followed. The government shortly charged Yukos with tax evasion and slapped the company with a $33 billion bill for back taxes—an amount larger than the combined tax bill for the entire oil industry. Khodorkovsky was arrested in October for fraud and tax evasion, and in the ensuing sham of a trial, he was sentenced to nine years in Siberian prison.

The government soon began dismantling the company. In December 2004, it auctioned Yukos's key asset, Yuganskneftegaz, which held the bulk of its oil reserves. The auction removed any semblance of doubt Putin was at work—the acquiring entity was an unknown company, Baikalfinansgrup, allegedly registered at the address of a hairdresser's salon in Tver.[36] The fictitious company was immediately sold to state-owned oil producer, Rosneft. In another auction, Yukos's glass and steel headquarters sold for $3.9 billion, despite estimates it couldn't be worth more than $250 million.[37] Similar auctions over other Yukos assets also raised eyebrows.

Ostensibly, the government was making it known it had no reservations stealing valuable assets for its own enrichment. The initial public offering (IPO) of Rosneft in 2006—the largest listing in Russian history, raising $10.4 billion—illustrated to the world the new paradigm of Russian markets, one where the state controlled markets and held a firm grip on power.[38] Indeed, the next several years saw the government repeatedly flexing its muscles, especially in renationalizing energy assets. Several joint ventures between Russian and Western oil companies were suspiciously shut down for environmental reasons. Other Western firms were told to surrender a controlling stake if they wished to remain in business. Though the state started with energy firms, many other sectors found themselves targets in the ensuing years.

Caveat Emptor

To understand the full implications of the return of Soviet-style authority, consider the story of Mechel, Russia's largest exporter of *coking* coal (a vital input into the steel-making process). An economic boom and massive infrastructure build-outs in emerging markets kept demand for such natural resources inordinately high from 2003 to 2007. Mechel smartly leveraged this demand by selling its coking coal into the more expensive foreign spot markets. It consistently posted exceptional earnings growth, and its share price soared.

But its actions angered the Russian steel sector, which wanted the company to enter into long-term contracts with domestic steel makers at a lower cost. Someone in the sector clearly had Putin's attention. Putin called a meeting with steel makers to discuss the situation, but Mechel's CEO was unable to attend due to heart problems. The perceived snub angered Putin. He called for Russia's antimonopoly organization to investigate Mechel for price-fixing and charged the company with tax evasion. At one point, the government considered adding criminal charges. Figure 4.3 plots Mechel's share price at the time. As you can see, Putin's attack cut the company's market value by

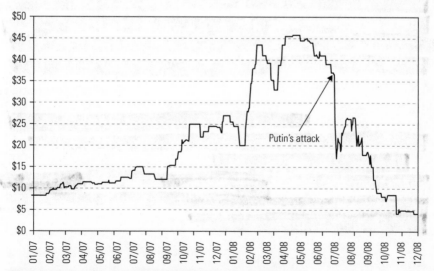

Putin's attack

Figure 4.3   Don't Mess With Mother Russia
Source: Thomson Datastream.

more than half in a mere two days—a stark reminder to foreign investors of Russia's inherent political risks.

From the outside, Mechel appeared guilty only of smart business sense. In freely functioning markets, a company is allowed to sell its goods at the highest price the market bears. Herein lies the most valuable lesson—Russia is not a true market. Years of heavy-handed recentralization under Putin changed the rules of the game, and property rights are tenuous at best. The government can single-handedly erase an investment position to zero in a flash. Caveat emptor.

Does this mean investors should avoid Russia entirely? Probably not. As we'll discuss in subsequent chapters, zero allocation to an important country like Russia means taking on a substantial amount of benchmark risk. Investors simply need to remain cognizant of Russia's history and political tendencies. Russian firms may appear to operate in a competitive market, and their managers may say they act independently. But they all work within a strategic framework ultimately dictated by the state and the legacies of its Soviet past.

THE LEGACY OF APARTHEID—RACE AND MARKETS

South Africa has a long and complicated racial history. European settlers in the seventeenth and eighteenth centuries colonized its coast for ports vital to trade with the East. These settlers enslaved many native Africans, beginning a trend of racial conflict that would last over three centuries, from the Zulu kingdom to the Boer Wars to apartheid (a set of laws allowing the ruling white minority to segregate and discriminate against the black majority). In no other corner of the world is the relationship between race and broader society as institutionalized as South Africa.

The end of apartheid in 1994 is a microcosm of this history. It bridged two worlds, leaving lasting inefficiencies while creating new ones. Apartheid and its aftermath teach us race can play a key role in shaping a country's investment climate.

Apartheid—A Brief History

Eighteenth-century South Africa was a melting pot of culture and race. Indigenous Africans mingled with Dutch, French, and German immigrants. The mixture was transformative—assimilation bred unique cultures and ideologies. The Afrikaners (also known as the Boers) were a group born from this period. Farmers of European descent, Afrikaners developed their own language (Afrikaans) and practiced a distinct form of fundamentalist Calvinism. Apartheid would be their lasting legacy.

Afrikaners originally settled around South Africa's coastal areas, but the arrival of the British at the end of the nineteenth century forced them into the northern reaches of the country. There, they successfully battled the Zulus, a dominant African tribe, establishing white superiority over the region. In the 1850s, the British granted independence to two Boer states—Transvaal and the Orange Free State. For the next several years, Afrikaners lived peacefully on their new land.

But the discovery of gold and diamonds in their territories put the Afrikaners in the direct path of British imperial might. The British mistakenly gave away a key asset and now they wanted it back. Tensions between the Afrikaners and British boiled over toward the end of the nineteenth century, leading to the Boer Wars. The British emerged victorious, but the brutality of the conflict created lasting implications.

Afrikaners were banished to industrialized urban areas and quickly fell into poverty. Once the owners of African slaves, Afrikaners now found themselves in direct competition with them for jobs—vast numbers of migrant black workers appeared in the settlements, offering to work in the mines cheaply. Afrikaners themselves were subjected to increasingly venomous racism by their Anglo peers. A strident nationalism was born from this suffering, laying the foundations for apartheid.

By the early to mid-twentieth century, a growing number of Afrikaner intellectuals began unfurling concepts supporting racial segregation. Calvinist religious leaders played a key role. They popularized the idea Afrikaners had the divine right to exist as a separate nation, free from the British model that forced them to assimilate as a minority among other ethnic groups. To preserve their culture and heritage, the Afrikaners felt they had no choice but to repress black development. From this, the leap to apartheid was easy. Racism begat racism.[39]

The nationalist Afrikaner National Party unexpectedly won South Africa's 1948 parliamentary elections. Race played a large role in governing society in the previous decades—there were already several laws on the books regulating blacks' ability to purchase land and what jobs they could hold. But Afrikaner nationalism brought about a complete social transformation along racial lines. Apartheid became their "manifest destiny," a way to cement white rule.

The main impetus for apartheid was political, but its methods were all-encompassing. Apartheid stripped away nearly every economic, political, and social liberty for all non-white citizens. Logistically, the system was based on a series of laws related to race. The first few touched aspects of social life, such as the marriage between different races. But they soon became increasingly restrictive and institutionalized—a flurry of acts passed by the Afrikaner legislature in the 1950s condemned blacks to second-class citizens. Here are some of the most impactful:

- **Population Registration Act (1950)**: Required all South Africans to be racially classified into one of three categories: white, black (African), or colored (mixed). Something as mundane as a person's habits, education, speech, or demeanor could be used as qualifying criteria.
- **Bantu Authorities Act (1951)**: Established "homelands" to which every non-white person was assigned and eventually deported. These were independent states, and all political rights were restricted to each person's homeland. To enter South Africa for any purpose (including work) required a passport.
- **Pass Laws Act (1952)**: Required all black South Africans to carry a "pass book" at all times. This book stipulated where, when, and for how long a person could remain in a specific area. The lack of a pass book was grounds for arrest and imprisonment.
- **Bantu Education Act (1953)**: Enforced racial segregation in all educational institutions. The law also led to a substantial reduction in government aid to already struggling black schools.[40]

Stories of brutality from the National Party's enforcement of these rules are too numerous and abhorrent to recount in their entirety.

Unsurprisingly, blacks fought back against their oppression, and uprisings were common. The African National Congress (ANC), the political party that supported black rights, rose in prominence and became a beacon of black support. But as the Sharpeville (1960) and Soweto (1976) massacres showed, the white government wouldn't give in easily—they had staked their livelihood on the success of the apartheid system.

If one looked past the blatant racism, however, apartheid capitalism seemed to work economically at first. In the first 30 years of National Party rule, the South African economy grew nearly 5 percent per year on average.[41] The country's deep supply of minerals and vast pool of cheap black labor fueled the growth boom. South Africa possesses some of the planet's largest deposits of gold, platinum, chromium, vanadium, and manganese, and it holds significant reserves of many others. In 1970, South Africa accounted for nearly 80 percent of the world's gold output.[42]

But abundant natural resources and steady economic growth hid deep-rooted problems. Apartheid was inherently at odds with economic progress. Blacks—the majority of the population—were economically and politically devastated. Not enough jobs were created to employ migrants from the homelands. The domestic consumer market struggled to grow with so many impoverished citizens. And institutionalized racism proved expensive—the government spent increasingly large sums to keep the economy moving despite constraints facing four-fifths of its population.

International forces also weighed on South Africa's economy. The end of the gold standard in 1971 meant the price for the country's key commodity now fluctuated wildly, depriving the government of a solid revenue base. The government's inward-looking policies soon squandered away windfall revenues from previously high, stable gold prices. More importantly, a strong distaste for apartheid's racism prompted governments around the world to impose significant economic sanctions on South Africa, blocking access to export markets, imports, and investment capital. This proved to be an economic death blow, and the economy began to falter—from 1982 to 1992, it barely grew 1 percent a year.[43] Without strong growth diverting attention from the country's entrenched problems, the ugliness of the apartheid system was exposed.

An increasingly large and vocal portion of South African society began publicly opposing the government's policies. After brutally resisting for decades, the white government finally relented. There was no seminal event, but the National Party began a peacemaking process with the African National Congress in the early 1990s. Negotiations lasted several years, and in 1994, the ANC won South Africa's first democratic elections—marking the official end to the apartheid era.

The Gold Standard

In 1944, representatives of 44 countries convened in Bretton Woods, New Hampshire, to discuss solutions to a wide variety of economic problems, such as the cost of rebuilding war-torn nations and the fostering of macroeconomic stability. Several iconic institutions were established that day, such as the International Monetary Fund, World Bank, and United Nations, but it was the creation of a new monetary regime—the Bretton Woods system, or *gold standard*—that would have the most impact.

Many believed the depression of the 1930s was partly a result of governments manipulating currencies to alter the natural flow of trade. As such, the attending nations agreed to fix their currency to the US dollar, which was backed by gold. One ounce of gold bullion equaled $35, and each country agreed to buy and sell US dollars to keep their currency within 1 percent of this exchange rate. In 1971, US President Richard Nixon was forced to end the gold standard as successive deficits ignited worries that dollar liabilities would be converted to gold at once. All the gold in Fort Knox was quite literally in jeopardy since it held only a third of the gold necessary to cover the amount of foreign-held dollars. The vast majority of the countries in the Bretton Woods regime then moved to the free float systems in place today.

Source: M.J. Stephey. A Brief History of Bretton Woods System. Time, October 21, 2008.

Apartheid's Aftermath

Apartheid left South Africa with dramatic structural problems. Blacks claimed no meaningful physical property, no shares in important businesses, no ownership over the political process. Simply put, South Africa was among the most unequal places on Earth at its end, the average per capita income for whites was about 9.5 times higher than for Africans, and well over half of blacks lived below the poverty line.[44]

A large part of this inequality stemmed from poor job prospects. Apartheid barred blacks from all but the most arduous and worst-paying jobs, and the education system deliberately kept them qualified for little else. The "color bar" meant there was no point to train blacks as professionals since it was illegal for companies to offer them such jobs anyway. These policies bequeathed a high supply of unskilled labor and a chronic shortage of skilled workers. This remains evident today, South Africa's official unemployment rate hovers around 25 percent.[45] The rate for blacks is likely substantially higher.

Labor inequality also gave rise to increasingly influential trade unions. When the ANC took power in 1994, it was in alliance with the Congress of South African Trade Unions (COSATU), the country's preeminent labor organization. To appease its power base, the ANC immediately embarked on a campaign to improve the labor environment. The rise of trade unions had unintended consequences, they shielded black workers from traditional market forces, making labor markets less flexible.

Apartheid also left a very concentrated ownership structure. In 1992, the top six conglomerates accounted for 85 percent of the Johannesburg Stock Exchange by market capitalization.[46] The Afrikaner ethos of self-reliance meant it wasn't just blacks that Afrikaners wanted no part of—this philosophy extended to the outside world as well. For example, the National Party employed exchange controls in 1961 prohibiting the convertibility of the rand, the country's currency. No company could expand internationally, so they did so horizontally instead, creating vast monoliths dominating the domestic economy. South African Breweries (SAB), for instance, controlled 98 percent of the country's beer market. With this market cornered, it diversified into furniture making, department stores, and watches.[47] This brewed inefficiencies—there are few synergies between beer and time pieces.

Black Economic Empowerment

Apartheid's most enduring legacy for investors was an affirmative action policy called Black Economic Empowerment (BEE). Conceptualized in the first several years after apartheid's end, its objective was simple: to redress the systematic exclusion of the majority of South Africans in the full participation of the economy. Few disagreed with its aims, but its implementation evoked widespread controversy.

At first, the government provided few guidelines for empowerment, leaving various arms of the state, private enterprise, and other interested parties to their own devices. Since apartheid deprived blacks of any modicum of wealth, banks began lending money to black consortia (BEE companies) to acquire shares in white businesses. These groups would purchase shares in return for voting rights. The banks in turn received the share performance, up to a certain rate, and anything beyond that went to the black consortia. But the logic behind this scheme was flawed—it capped the bank's return on the upside, yet they remained responsible for all the downside. Inappropriate risk-taking by the BEE companies ensued, and when markets turned sour in the late 1990s, many of these consortia collapsed.

Recognizing the need for a broader, more formalized approach, the government vetted ideas among politicians, the business community, and Africans. In September 2003, South Africa's parliament ratified the Broad-Based Black Economic Empowerment (B-BBEE). President Thabo Mbeki signed the bill into law in January 2004—affirmative action was now officially institutionalized.

The legislative framework relied on "scorecards," like Table 4.1, to evaluate every South African company on seven factors. Firms were assessed on the level of black ownership, the color of the managers and staff, their degree of assistance to black entrepreneurs, training provided to black workers, the amount spent on black social programs, and to what extent their supply chain was also "empowered."[48] Many industries also published additional criteria specific to their businesses.

A company's BEE "score" has widespread implications. BEE is mandatory only for government or state-owned companies. But companies

Table 4.1   The BEE Scorecard

Core Component of BEE	Indicators	Conversion Factor	Raw Score	Weighting	Total Score
Direct Empowerment Score					
Equity Ownership	% share of economic benefits			20%	
Management	% black persons in executive management and/or executive board and board committees			10%	
Human Resource Development and Employment Equity Score					
Employment Equity	Weighted employment equity analysis			10%	
Skills Development	Skills development expenditure as a proportion of total procurement			20%	
Indirect Empowerment Score					
Preferential Procurement	Procurement from black-owned and empowered enterprises as a proportion of total procurement			20%	
Enterprise Development	Investment in black-owned and empowered enterprises as a proportion of total assets			10%	
Residual 10%					
To Be Determined by Sector/Enterprise				10%	
Total Score out of 100%					

Source: Department of Trade and Industry (DTI).

ignore the system at their own peril—non-compliance means potentially losing out on key licenses or government contracts. Good empowerment credentials are pretty much required for those wishing to do business with the government.

South Africa's Anglo Platinum, the world's largest producer of platinum, illustrates this struggle. An industry BEE charter stripped mining rights from companies and put them into state hands. Mining companies like Anglo Platinum had to reapply for "new" rights within five years, and the government's process for granting new rights included several BEE requirements, such as the transfer of 26 percent ownership to blacks by 2014.[49] Anglo Platinum worked on its compliance, but the government accused it of being too slow. Only in February 2008, after several years of wrangling, did the company finally receive new order mining rights. Anglo Platinum's long-running spat with the government adversely affected their expansion plans.

BEE legislation also created several other inefficiencies. Critics complain BEE is rooted in cronyism—that only a small lucky and well-connected few have benefited. In addition, initial empowerment deals were rooted in the taking over of existing enterprises, not the creation of new ones, translating into fewer jobs for the black masses. More broadly, the policy adds operational costs for companies through such things as legal fees and share-price discounts. One estimate puts the additional cost at approximately 3 percent of stock market capitalization for the first 10 percent of capital transferred to new black owners.[50]

BEE policies also scare away foreign investors. In 2007, three Italian mining companies filed an international lawsuit demanding $350 million in compensation for mines the government seized in its BEE initiative.[51] Weak property rights hardly instill investor confidence.

Most importantly, BEE allowed the government to circumvent market forces and redistribute wealth through a spate of instruments—legislation, regulation, preferential treatment, institutional and financial support, and partnerships with the private sector. Such action has enduring consequences for investors. For instance, a perfectly qualified company may lose out on a government project because it did not spend enough on social programs to help blacks or failed to meet a hiring quota.

The ANC's rise to power did not symbolize the end of South Africa's relationship between race and capitalism, but the beginning of a new chapter. Affirmative action added new layers of complexity to markets, and BEE amounted to forced wealth redistribution, similar in spirit to the Latin American populist polices described in Chapter 3. Few can argue against the need for redress for blacks after decades of brutally enforced racism. But for markets, which are our primary focus, such policies are anathema.

Chapter Recap

The collapse of the Soviet Union is a fascinating case study in capital markets history. From the remnants of communism and a centrally planned economy, a new style of capitalism was born—a wild, wild East, learned on the fly. Not surprisingly, it was a tumultuous period for Russians and investors alike, culminating in the 1998 financial crisis that left the country broke and battered.

- Russia's quick recovery from that crisis owes much to Vladimir Putin.
  - Yet he brought the country nearly full circle with the ideologies of its Soviet past, nationalizing key energy and materials assets—and wielding influence over many others.
  - His rule dramatically altered the country's investment landscape. Today, Russian markets are less "market" than a medium for political power.
- South Africa also presents a unique case for investors—race and markets are intertwined.
  - Decades of race-based rule under apartheid left severe economic dislocations the country still struggles with today.
  - However, the policies adopted to redress these inequalities have only made investing in the region more complicated and fraught with inefficiencies.

II

DEVELOPING AN EMERGING MARKETS STRATEGY

5

FROM THE PAST TO TODAY—HOW TO APPROACH EMERGING MARKETS

History provides valuable context—if we started with a blank page, investing would be largely guesswork. An evaluation of the present should always and everywhere be grounded in probabilities using the past as context. The preceding chapters provided the relevant structure. But that only gets you halfway. Markets are constantly evolving and changing before our very eyes—no two periods are exactly the same. Investors must interpret the events of yesterday into a relevant framework for today. To begin building an emerging markets portfolio, we need an understanding of its composition today. In this chapter, we deconstruct the current emerging market landscape to gain a better understanding of the areas most important to investors. We then provide a framework for thinking about markets—the top-down method—further detailing the important steps in Chapters 6 and 7.

PRELUDE TO A PORTFOLIO: CHOOSING A BENCHMARK

Investors often say their goal is to beat the "market," but they rarely identify what market they mean. Yet you can't successfully beat a market unless you choose a specific one to beat. Thus, before building any portfolio, investors must choose a benchmark.

A benchmark is your market. It's an index tracking whatever asset class(es) you wish to invest in. As discussed in Chapter 1, there are indexes designed to track every imaginable investment, from US Midwestern real estate values to the probability of default for corporate bonds. Most investors are familiar with indexes as a way to track general market performance, but very few use them as benchmarks. This is misguided, as benchmarks serve several critical functions.

A Performance Yardstick

If your portfolio was down 10 percent in one year, did you do well? Most investors would answer a resounding no—no one likes to lose money. But there isn't enough information here to appropriately answer the question. What if we told you the broader market fell 30 percent over the same period? In that environment, a 10 percent decline sounds pretty good. Similarly, if your portfolio rose 10 percent but the broader market was up 30 percent, you aren't likely to be too happy. Too often, investors focus on *absolute* return. But a better focus is *relative* return. Rather than maximizing return in the short run, your portfolio management goal should be maximizing the likelihood of beating your benchmark. Beating a properly constructed benchmark consistently over a long period of time by even a modest amount should afford you great investment success.

A Roadmap

Most investors think the ultimate goal of managing money is maximizing return. Not so. This is akin to thinking the best way to drive across the country is to keep the gas pedal to the floor the entire time. You might get ahead in the straight-aways, but the first obstacle can quickly send you veering off course. Most rational drivers use a roadmap to plan the quickest and safest route. A benchmark does the same for your investments by guiding your portfolio construction. Its components tell you what to include and in what percentage.

Say your benchmark is the MSCI Emerging Markets Index. Turkey represents 1.5 percent of the total index by market capitalization. Using this weight as a guide, you can either *overweight, underweight,* or *neutral weight* Turkey relative to the benchmark. Being *overweight* means owning more Turkish stocks by weight than the benchmark. An underweight is the exact opposite—owning less than the benchmark. And a neutral weight means your Turkish weight is in line with the benchmark. Generally speaking, investors seek to overweight categories they expect to outperform their benchmark and underweight those they believe will not.

Note that being pessimistic on a country doesn't necessarily mean holding zero weight to that country. Instead, it might only mean holding a lesser percentage than the benchmark. This is an important feature of benchmarking—it allows an investor to make strategic decisions on sectors and countries, but maintains diversification, thus managing risk more appropriately.

Benchmark Risk

In the long run, the greatest risk you take as an investor is *benchmark risk*, or how much your portfolio differs from the benchmark in a specific component. For example, think of investors who bought into the technology phenomenon in the late 1990s. Many investors allowed their allocation to the sector to creep up well beyond the market weight—about 30 percent of the S&P 500 then—to 60, even 90 percent of their portfolio. With such a big relative weight, these investors were taking on an inordinate amount of benchmark risk. While they realized stellar returns for a while, they were hurt badly when technology stocks imploded.

Source: Thomson Datastream.

Benchmark weights also determine the relative impact a country (or any other benchmark component) has on the overall index's performance. For example, a 2 percent return in China (weight 18.2 percent in the MSCI Emerging Markets Index) matters more to overall performance than a 20 percent return in Turkey, because China is over 12 times the weight in the index.[1]

Calculating Portfolio Performance

Imagine a three-stock portfolio, consisting of Stocks A, B, and C. Stock A is 20 percent of the portfolio, Stock B 30 percent, and Stock C the remaining 50 percent. If Stock A returned 10 percent, Stock B 20 percent, and Stock C minus 20 percent, what is the portfolio's return?

1	2	3	4
			Contribution to
Stock	Weight	Return	Return
A	20%	10%	2%
B	30%	20%	6%
C	50%	−20%	−10%
	Portfolio Return (Sum of Column 4)		*−2%*

To calculate the return for the entire portfolio, we must compute the *weighted return*, or portfolio contribution, for each stock. This is as simple as multiplying each stock's weight by its return (Column 2 × Column 3). The sum of each stock's contribution is the total portfolio. In this example, the large weight of Stock C leads to a negative portfolio return, outweighing the appreciation of Stocks A and B.

The same concepts apply to any other "breakdown" of your portfolio—by sector, country, etc. As long as you can assign a weight and a return to a component, you can calculate its contribution to overall performance. This is a common way to evaluate your performance.

Last, benchmark weights are not static—they change over time based on each index component's performance. The biggest sector or country today won't necessarily be the biggest next year (again, see technology's bust in the early 2000s). As such, it's crucial to periodically monitor these weights to ensure your portfolio is properly aligned.

Supporting or Leading Role?

As you can see, picking a benchmark is no small consideration—whichever one you choose will have lasting implications on the makeup of your portfolio and how you evaluate your success. By picking up this book, we assume you're already well attuned to the wonders of global investing and need no convincing of its merits (if not, see Aaron Anderson's *Own the World*). But the goals and objectives of every global investor are different, and emerging markets' role varies along with them. So what benchmark is appropriate for emerging markets investors?

There are essentially two answers to this question, depending on whether you want emerging markets to play a supporting or leading role. If you're adding emerging markets to a pre-existing global, developed market benchmark like the MSCI World Index, you'll want to switch your index to one that includes emerging markets. The MSCI All-Country World Index (ACWI) is an appropriately broad, well-constructed index covering both developed and emerging markets (remember, we reference MSCI in this book, but any number of index providers create suitable indexes; the criteria across providers are essentially the same). However, if you intend to manage emerging markets as a standalone portfolio, you'll want to choose a benchmark consisting only of emerging markets stocks, like the MSCI Emerging Markets Index.

Which one you choose is essentially a question of weight. A global investor benchmarked to the MSCI ACWI will have a substantially smaller allocation to emerging markets than one devoted solely to the asset class. At year-end 2008, emerging markets represented nearly 10 percent of the MSCI ACWI.[2] Obviously, if you benchmarked to the MSCI Emerging Markets Index, your portfolio would consist entirely of emerging market stocks.

This may seem overly straightforward, but there are subtle implications. A global investor should be less concerned with the smaller emerging markets weights. Take our earlier Turkey example. If you're managing a standalone emerging markets portfolio, you might pay some attention to the country given its 1.5 percent weight. Not huge, but not completely insignificant. However, if the MSCI ACWI is your benchmark, Turkey comprises only a tiny fraction—0.2 percent. A weight that small isn't going to have too much of an impact on your overall performance and can largely be ignored. In either case, you've presumably made the decision to invest *some* money in emerging markets. An evaluation of the asset classes today is thus appropriate for both types of investors.

GETTING STARTED: EMERGING MARKETS TODAY

With your benchmark in hand, it's time to turn to emerging markets. What does the asset class look like today? Investors who follow the major financial publications may believe it starts and ends with Brazil, Russia, India, and China, known as the BRICs. These markets command the bulk of headlines.

But while these countries are undoubtedly important to your portfolio's performance, their reputation is partly successful marketing. Take a guess at the five largest emerging markets by market capitalization. You probably correctly picked China at the top of the list. That's an easy one. But we bet most readers wouldn't guess South Korea, Taiwan, and South Africa come before Russia or India on the

Table 5.1   MSCI Emerging Markets Index Country Weights

Country	Weight	Country	Weight
China	18.2%	Indonesia	1.5%
South Korea	13.6%	Chile	1.4%
Brazil	12.9%	Thailand	1.4%
Taiwan	10.9%	Czech Republic	0.9%
South Africa	8.4%	Egypt	0.7%
India	6.5%	Peru	0.7%
Russia	5.7%	Colombia	0.6%
Mexico	5.2%	Hungary	0.6%
Israel	3.4%	Morocco	0.5%
Malaysia	3.0%	Philippines	0.5%
Poland	1.6%	Argentina	0.1%
Turkey	1.5%	Pakistan	0.1%

Source: Thomson Datastream, MSCI, Inc.[3] as of 12/31/2008.

scale of relative size. Table 5.1 shows the breakdown weights of the MSCI Emerging Markets Index by country as of December 31, 2008.

From a sector standpoint, the distribution is more evenly spread. Financials is by far the largest, but virtually every sector is substantial enough to warrant some attention (see Table 5.2).

GICS

The 10 sectors listed in Table 5.2 represent the *Global Industry Classification System* (GICS), a system of placing stocks into similar sector and industry categories. For example, the Consumer Staples sector consists of companies less sensitive to the economic cycle— it includes food, beverages, tobacco, and personal care products. GICS was developed by MSCI and Standard & Poor's. Other index providers use slightly different formats. While the nomenclature and categories are slightly different, the concepts remain the same. Any of the major emerging markets indexes introduced in Chapter 1 are entirely acceptable.

Source: Standard and Poor's, "GICS Sector Descriptions," (August 29, 2008).

Combining the two categories together—sector and country—we get Table 5.3, which reveals how sector weights vary by country. For example, Telecommunication Services represents nearly 25 percent of

Table 5.2   MSCI Emerging Markets Sector Weights

Sector	Weight
Financials	22.8%
Energy	14.9%
Telecommunication Services	13.6%
Materials	12.8%
Information Technology	10.8%
Industrials	7.7%
Consumer Staples	5.8%
Consumer Discretionary	4.8%
Utilities	4.0%
Health Care	2.9%

Source: Thomson Datastream, MSCI, Inc.[4] as of 12/31/2008.

Table 5.3 Emerging Market Country-Sector Intersections

Country	Consumer Discretionary	Consumer Staples	Energy	Financials	Health Care	Industrials	Information Technology	Materials	Telecom	Utilities	Total
Argentina	0.0%		0.0%	0.0%				0.0%	0.0%		**0.1%**
Brazil	0.4%	0.7%	3.5%	2.8%		0.3%	0.2%	3.3%	0.7%	1.0%	**12.9%**
Chile	0.0%	0.2%		0.1%		0.2%		0.3%	0.1%	0.5%	**1.4%**
China	0.6%	0.7%	3.3%	6.0%		1.7%	0.5%	0.8%	4.2%	0.4%	**18.2%**
Colombia	0.0%		0.2%	0.2%				0.1%		0.1%	**0.6%**
Czech Republic	0.0%			0.1%	0.1%			0.0%	0.1%	0.5%	**0.9%**
Egypt				0.2%		0.2%		0.1%	0.3%		**0.7%**
Hungary			0.2%	0.2%	0.1%				0.1%		**0.6%**
India	0.2%	0.5%	1.3%	1.6%	0.3%	0.6%	0.9%	0.5%	0.2%	0.4%	**6.5%**
Indonesia	0.1%	0.1%	0.1%	0.5%		0.0%		0.1%	0.4%	0.1%	**1.5%**
Israel			0.0%	0.3%	2.2%	0.1%	0.3%	0.3%	0.2%		**3.4%**
Korea	1.3%	1.0%	0.4%	2.2%	0.1%	2.6%	3.2%	1.6%	0.8%	0.4%	**13.6%**
Malaysia	0.4%	0.5%	0.0%	0.9%		0.6%		0.0%	0.2%	0.4%	**3.0%**
Mexico	0.7%	1.2%		0.2%		0.3%		0.6%	2.3%		**5.2%**

Morocco	0.0%	0.1%		0.3%		0.1%				0.2%	**0.5%**
Pakistan			0.0%	0.0%				0.0%		0.0%	**0.1%**
Peru				0.2%				0.5%			**0.7%**
Philippines	0.0%			0.2%		0.0%				0.2%	**0.5%**
Poland	0.1%		0.3%	0.9%		0.1%	0.0%	0.1%		0.3%	**1.6%**
Russia	0.0%	0.0%	3.7%	0.5%	0.0%			0.6%		0.7%	**5.7%**
South Africa	0.8%	0.4%	1.0%	2.1%	0.1%	0.4%		2.2%		1.3%	**8.4%**
Taiwan	0.2%	0.2%	0.1%	1.9%		0.4%	5.7%	1.5%		0.8%	**10.9%**
Thailand	0.0%		0.6%	0.4%		0.0%		0.1%		0.2%	**1.4%**
Turkey	0.0%	0.1%	0.1%	0.8%		0.1%		0.1%		0.3%	**1.5%**
Total	*4.8%*	*5.8%*	*14.9%*	*22.8%*	*2.9%*	*7.7%*	*10.8%*	*12.8%*	*13.6%*	*4.0%*	*100.0%*

Source: Thomson Datastream, MSCI, Inc.[5] as of 12/31/2008.

China (4.2 percent divided by 18.2 percent), but in Brazil, it's barely 5 percent (0.7 percent divided by 12.9 percent). Also, not every country contains every sector—going fishing in the Philippines for a Materials stock will leave you empty-handed. Given these idiosyncrasies, a brief breakdown of the major regions is appropriate.

Regional Landscape

The MSCI Emerging Markets Index comprises three regions: Europe, the Middle East & Africa (EMEA), Latin America, and Asia. At year end 2008, 21 percent of the index was in Latin America, 23 percent in EMEA, and 56 percent in Asia.[6] Each region has a distinct composition.

Emerging Asia

Emerging Asia is the largest region by market capitalization, consisting of nine countries (in order of weight): China, Korea, Taiwan, India, Malaysia, Indonesia, Thailand, Philippines, and Pakistan. Financials is the largest sector in the region, followed by Information Technology and Telecommunication Services.

Table 5.4   Emerging Asia Sector Weights

Sector	Weight in MSCI EM	Weight in EM Asia
Financials	13.8%	24.8%
Information Technology	10.3%	18.5%
Telecommunication Services	7.0%	12.6%
Energy	5.9%	10.6%
Industrials	5.9%	10.6%
Materials	4.6%	8.3%
Consumer Staples	3.1%	5.5%
Consumer Discretionary	2.8%	5.0%
Utilities	1.9%	3.4%
Health Care	0.4%	0.6%
Total	**55.7%**	**100.0%**

Source: Thomson Datastream, MSCI Inc.[7] as of 12/31/2008.

Europe, Middle East & Africa (EMEA)

The second largest region, EMEA, also has nine countries (in order of weight): South Africa, Russia, Israel, Poland, Turkey, Czech Republic, Egypt, Hungary, and Morocco. Financials is again the largest sector, but EMEA has virtually no exposure to Information Technology stocks. Instead, it also has a notable weight to Energy (see Table 5.5).

Latin America

Latin America is the smallest emerging market region, both by number of countries and weight. It consists of (in order of weight): Brazil, Mexico, Chile, Peru, Colombia, and Argentina. Latin America's sector weights are quite different than the other regions. The Materials and Energy sectors account for 40 percent. At the other end of the spectrum, the region has miniscule exposure to Information Technology and none to Health Care (see Table 5.6).

Taking all this together, some initial thoughts on portfolio construction should be forming in your head. If you thought Information Technology will outperform in the period ahead, what region would you

Table 5.5   Europe, Middle East & Africa Sector Weights

Sector	Weight in MSCI EM	Weight in EM EMEA
Financials	5.3%	22.8%
Energy	5.2%	22.4%
Telecommunication Services	3.5%	14.8%
Materials	3.4%	14.5%
Health Care	2.5%	10.8%
Industrials	1.0%	4.2%
Consumer Discretionary	0.9%	3.9%
Consumer Staples	0.6%	2.6%
Utilities	0.6%	2.5%
Information Technology	0.3%	1.3%
Total	**23.3%**	**100.0%**

Source: Thomson Datastream, MSCI, Inc.8 as of 12/31/2008.

Table 5.6   Latin America Sector Weights

Sector	Weight in MSCI EM	Weight in EM LatAm
Materials	4.7%	22.6%
Energy	3.7%	17.7%
Financials	3.7%	17.4%
Telecommunication Services	3.1%	15.0%
Consumer Staples	2.1%	10.1%
Utilities	1.5%	7.3%
Consumer Discretionary	1.1%	5.2%
Industrials	0.8%	4.0%
Information Technology	0.2%	0.8%
Health Care	0.0%	0.0%
Total	**21.0%**	**100.0%**

Source: Thomson Datastream, MSCI, Inc.[9]

look to first? Or what region might you avoid if you expected Materials or Energy stocks to decline? We'll cover this in a bit more detail in ensuing chapters, but it's important to keep these considerations in mind when thinking about your approach.

THE BEST WAY TO THINK ABOUT EMERGING MARKETS

The preceding overview of the current landscape reveals an important theme: Emerging markets are very concentrated. A few countries dominate the market, and those countries are dominated by a few sectors and a handful of stocks. This concept is consistent with a broader way of thinking about portfolio management, an approach we believe offers investors the best chance for long-term success.

A Few Countries Dominate the Market

Take a peek at Table 5.1 again. Note its top-heavy structure. There may be 24 countries in the MSCI Emerging Markets Index, but only a handful have any real significance. For example, at less than one-tenth of a percent of the index weight, Argentina matters little to any properly managed portfolio. By contrast, countries like China, Korea, and South Africa are crucial to relative portfolio performance. Figure 5.1 illustrates this concept graphically. The top three countries make up 45 percent of the index. A mere 10 countries—less than half the total—represent nearly 90 percent of the index.[10]

This has broad implications. The vast majority of your time should be spent on a handful or two of countries. There may be individual winners at the stock level in some of the smaller countries such as Pakistan or Morocco. And events in these countries may reverberate through to other emerging markets. But following 24 countries with the same degree of detail is time-consuming and complicated. More importantly, these smaller countries are by definition not crucial to long-term success. So unless it's a particular interest of yours, you can track most emerging markets countries at arm's length. Focus your time on the largest countries—the decision to overweight or underweight them will have the greatest impact on your portfolio's relative performance.

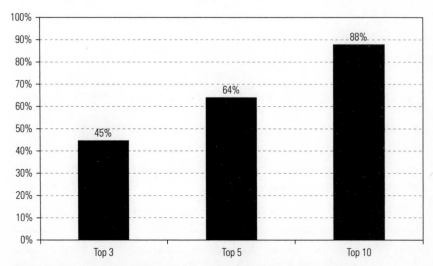

Figure 5.1   A Few Countries Dominate the Market
Source: Thomson Datastream, MSCI, Inc.[11] as of 12/31/2008.

Countries Are Concentrated, Too

Each country is also concentrated. As shown in Figure 5.2, the two largest sectors often represent a sizeable portion of the total market (in Peru's case, the *entire* market). This means an allocation to a specific country often has a residual allocation to the sectors that dominate it. For example, if you wish to purchase a Russian company, there's a good chance it will be in the Energy or Telecommunication Services sector. This also works the other way—if your interest is an Energy company, there's a good chance you'll eventually knock on Russia's door. Sometimes portfolio decisions will be driven by sector considerations; other times they will be driven by country considerations. Most of the time, however, it's some combination of both.

As Figure 5.3 shows, a handful of stocks comprise the bulk of most countries, too. The top five companies in Indonesia, for instance, make up nearly two-thirds of its market weight. Some corners of the world, like Argentina, don't even have five companies included in the index (it has four). By contrast, developed markets are notably less concentrated—the top five companies in the US and Japan comprise less than 15 percent of their respective countries.

The lesson? The structural characteristics of emerging markets reveal the best way to approach investing: from the top-down. Focusing solely on stocks, without considering underlying country or sector concentrations, can subject a portfolio to unintended performance swings.

PUTTING IT TOGETHER: THE TOP-DOWN METHOD

Overwhelmingly, investment professionals today do what can broadly be labeled "bottom-up" investing. Their emphasis is on stock selection. A typical bottom-up investor researches an assortment of companies and attempts to pick those with the greatest likelihood of outperforming the market. The type of stock is usually an afterthought—it could be a donut chain or lawn mower manufacturer as long as the company's individual merits warrant investment. The selected securities are cobbled together to form a portfolio, and factors like country and economic sector exposure are often residuals of security selection, not planned decisions.

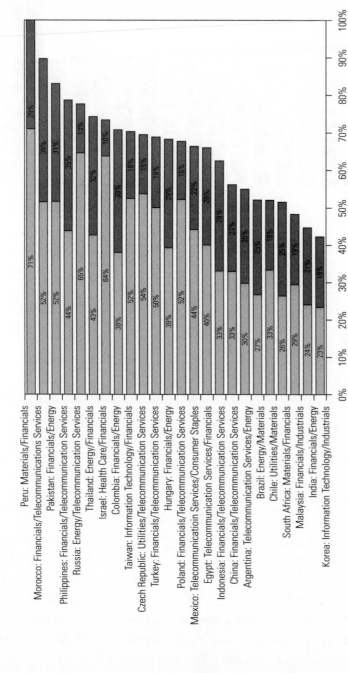

Figure 5.2 Sector Concentration Within Countries

Source: Thomson Datastream, MSCI Inc.[12] as of 12/31/2008.

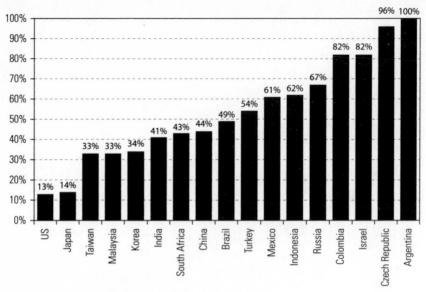

Figure 5.3   Five Stocks Make the Country
Source: Thomson Datastream, MSCI Inc.[13] as of 12/31/2008.

"Top-down" investing reverses the order. A top-down investor first analyzes big-picture factors like economics, politics, and sentiment to forecast which investment categories are most likely to outperform the market. Only then does a top-down investor begin looking at individual securities. Top-down investing is inevitably more concerned with a portfolio's aggregate exposure to investment categories than with any individual security. Thus, top-down is an inherently dynamic mode of investment because investment strategies are based upon the prevailing market and economic environment (which changes often).

There's significant debate in the investment community as to which approach is superior. This book's goal is not to reject bottom-up investing—there are indeed investors who've successfully utilized bottom-up approaches. Rather, the goal is to introduce a comprehensive and flexible methodology that any investor could use to build a portfolio designed to beat the global stock market in any investment environment. It's a framework for gleaning new insights and making good on information not already reflected in stock prices.

There are several key reasons why a top-down approach is advantageous:

- **Scalability**: A bottom-up process is akin to looking for needles in a haystack. A top-down process is akin to seeking the haystacks with the highest concentration of needles. Globally, there are 25,000+ publicly traded stocks. Even the largest institutions with the greatest research resources cannot hope to adequately examine all these companies. Smaller institutions and individual investors must prioritize where to focus their limited resources. Unlike a bottom-up process, a top-down process makes this gargantuan task manageable by determining, upfront, what slices of the market to examine at the security level.
- **Enhanced stock selection**: Well-designed top-down processes generate insights that can greatly enhance stock selection. Macroeconomic or political analysis, for instance, can help determine what types of firms will face head- or tailwinds (see Chapter 6 for a full explanation).
- **Risk control**: Bottom-up processes are highly subject to unintended risk concentrations. Top-down processes are inherently better suited to manage risk exposures throughout the investment process.
- **Macro overview**: Top-down processes are more conducive to avoiding macro-driven calamities like the bursting of the Japan bubble in the 1990s, the Technology bubble in 2000, or the bear market of 2000 to 2002. No matter how good an individual company may be, it is still beholden to sector, regional, and broad market factors. In fact, there is evidence "macro" factors can largely determine a stock's performance regardless of individual merit.

Top-Down Means Thinking 70-20-10

A top-down investment process also helps focus on what's most important to investment results: asset allocation and sub-asset allocation decisions. Many investors focus most of their attention on security-level

portfolio decisions, like picking individual stocks they think will perform well. However, studies have shown that over 90 percent of return
variability is derived from asset allocation decisions, not market timing
or stock selection.[14]

Our research shows about 70 percent of return variability is derived
from asset allocation, 20 percent from sub-asset allocation (such as country, sector, size, and style), and 10 percent from security selection. While
security selection can make a significant difference over time, higher-level
portfolio decisions dominate investment results more often than not.

TOP-DOWN DECONSTRUCTED

The top-down method begins by first analyzing the macro environment.
It asks the "big" questions like: Do you think stocks will go up or down
in the next 12 months? If so, which countries or sectors should benefit most? Once you have decided on these high-level "themes," you can
examine various macro portfolio drivers to make general overweight and
underweight decisions for countries, sectors, industries, and sub-industries versus your benchmark.

For instance, let's say we've determined a macroeconomic driver that
goes something like this: "In the next 12 months, I believe global economic growth will be higher than most expect." That's a very high-level
statement with important implications for your portfolio. It means
you'd want to search for countries, industries, and ultimately stocks that
would benefit most from strong global economic growth. Chapter 6 will
cover the process of developing these types of portfolio drivers in depth.

The second step in top-down is applying quantitative screening
criteria to narrow the choice set of stocks. Since, in our hypothetical
example, we believe global growth will be strong, it likely means we're
bullish on emerging market stocks. But which ones? Are you bullish
on, say, mining companies? Department stores? Telephone carriers?
Do you want producers with exposure to a specific region? Do you
want small cap companies or large cap? And what about valuations?
Are you looking for growth or value? (Size and growth/value categories are often referred to as "style" decisions.) These criteria and more
can help you narrow the list of stocks you might buy.

There are thousands and thousands of stocks out there, so it's vital to use a series of factors like market capitalization and valuations to narrow the field a bit. Securities passing this screen are then subjected to further quantitative analysis to eliminate companies with excessive risk profiles relative to their peer group, such as companies with excessive leverage or balance sheet risk and securities lacking sufficient liquidity for investment.

The rigidity of the quantitative screens is entirely up to you and will determine the number of companies on your prospect list. The more rigid the criteria, the fewer the companies that make the list. Broader criteria will increase them.

EXAMPLES OF QUANTITATIVE FACTOR SCREENINGS

How can you perform such a screen? Here are two examples of quantitative factor screenings to show how broad or specific you can be. You might want to apply very strict criteria, or you may prefer to be broader.

Strict Criteria

- First, you decide you want to search for only emerging market companies. By definition, that excludes all companies from the developed markets. Already, you've narrowed the field a lot!
- Now, let's say, based on your high-level drivers, you only want Latin American stocks. By excluding all other regions besides Latin America, you've narrowed the field even more.
- Next, let's decide to search only for steel companies because you think demand for building materials will be high.
- Perhaps you don't believe very small stocks are preferable, so you limit market capitalization to $5 billion and above.
- Last, let's set some parameters for valuation:
  - P/E (price-to-earnings) less than 12
  - P/B (price-to-book) less than 8
  - P/CF (price-to-cash-flow) less than 10
  - P/S (price-to-sales) less than 10

This rigorous process of selecting parameters will yield a small number of stocks to research, all based on your higher-level themes. But maybe you have reason to be less specific and want to do a broader screen because you think emerging markets in general is a good place to be.

Broad Criteria

- Emerging markets
- Latin America (no sector restrictions)
- Market caps above $10 billion

This selection process is much broader and obviously gives you a much longer list of stocks to choose from.

Doing either a strict or broad screen isn't inherently better. It just depends on how well-formed and specific your higher-level themes are. Obviously, a stricter screen means less work for you in step three—actual stock selection.

After narrowing the prospect list, the third and final step is identifying individual securities possessing strategic attributes consistent with higher-level portfolio themes (Chapter 7 will cover the stock selection process in more detail). Your stock selection process should attempt to accomplish two goals:

1. Find firms possessing strategic attributes consistent with higher-level portfolio themes, derived from the drivers that give those firms a competitive advantage versus their peers. For example, if you believe owning firms with dominant market shares in consolidating industries is a favorable characteristic, you would search for firms with that profile.

2. Maximize the likelihood of beating the category of stocks you are analyzing. For example, if you want a certain portfolio weight to commercial banks and need 4 stocks out of 12 meeting the quantitative criteria, you then pick the 4 that, as a group, maximize the likelihood of beating all 12 as a whole. This is different than trying to pick "the best four." By avoiding stocks likely to be extreme or "weird" outliers versus the group, you can reduce portfolio risk while adding value at the security selection level.

In lieu of picking individual securities, there are other ways to exploit high-level themes in the top-down process. For instance, if you feel strongly about a particular sub-industry but don't think you can add value through individual security analysis, it may be more prudent to buy a group of companies in the sub-industry or a category product like an exchange-traded fund (ETF). There are a growing variety of ETFs that track the emerging markets. This way, you can be sure to gain broad exposure without much stock-specific risk. (For more information on ETFs, visit www.ishares.com, www.sectorspdr .com, or www.masterdata.com.)

Notice that a great deal of thinking, analysis, and work is done before you ever think about individual stocks. That's the key to the top-down approach: It emphasizes high-level themes and funnels its way down to individual stocks, as illustrated in Figure 5.4.

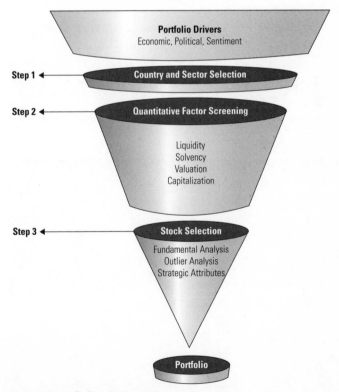

Figure 5.4   Portfolio Drivers

The next two chapters expand on Steps 1 and 3—the meat of the portfolio construction process—specifically in relation to emerging markets. We seek to provide the tools to answer the following types of questions: What allocation to emerging markets is appropriate? When might Latin American stocks outperform? How about Taiwan Health Care stocks (trick question, there are none in the index)?[15]

Chapter Recap

- Investing in emerging markets begins with an understanding of the category's composition. Consisting of three major regions—Europe, Middle East & Africa (EMEA), Latin America, and Asia—emerging markets are concentrated. Just a few countries, sectors, and stocks dominate the category.
- This concentration reveals the best way to approach investing: from the top-down.
- The top-down approach emphasizes big-picture factors like economics, politics, and sentiment to forecast which categories are most likely to outperform the market.
- These high-level themes—portfolio drivers—then funnel down to individual stock selection.

DEVELOPING PORTFOLIO DRIVERS

Portfolio drivers are the foundation of the top-down method. All subsequent portfolio decisions—country, sector, style, and security—stem from these higher level themes. Thus, accurately identifying current and future drivers is critical to success. In this chapter, we'll teach you to evaluate market conditions, aided by the knowledge and context accumulated in preceding chapters, to develop portfolio drivers for emerging markets. By developing and analyzing portfolio drivers you can better determine the market most likely to outperform or underperform your benchmark (i.e., the broader stock market) and allocate your portfolio appropriately.

THE IMPORTANCE OF PORTFOLIO DRIVERS IN EMERGING MARKETS

Despite some categorical similarities, emerging market countries are a diverse lot. Previous chapters provided a glimpse into these differences, but one only needs to open the newspaper to quickly appreciate the diversity across the category. Political models, economic composition, and social norms vary widely. Not surprisingly, market performance is equally disparate—both country and sector performance vary widely year to year. This underlines the importance of correctly identifying portfolio drivers.

Table 6.1 shows the best- and worst-performing countries in emerging markets and the spread between them each year since 1988. There are two important takeaways from the data. First, the difference between

Table 6.1   Best- and Worst-Performing Emerging Market Country by Year

Year	Best Country	Return	Worst Country	Return	Spread
1988	Indonesia	228%	Turkey	−63%	291%
1989	Turkey	472%	South Korea	0%	471%
1990	Mexico	59%	Brazil	−66%	124%
1991	Argentina	402%	Indonesia	−46%	448%
1992	Philippines	37%	Turkey	−50%	87%
1993	Poland	745%	Israel	14%	731%
1994	Brazil	64%	Poland	−55%	119%
1995	Peru	22%	Pakistan	−38%	60%
1996	Russia	151%	South Korea	−38%	189%
1997	Russia	112%	Indonesia	−75%	186%
1998	Korea	138%	Russia	−83%	221%
1999	Russia	246%	Colombia	−19%	265%
2000	Israel	25%	Indonesia	−63%	88%
2001	Russia	53%	Egypt	−44%	97%
2002	Pakistan	151%	Argentina	−51%	201%
2003	Thailand	144%	Malaysia	27%	117%
2004	Colombia	132%	Thailand	−1%	134%
2005	Egypt	162%	Malaysia	2%	159%
2006	China	83%	Turkey	−7%	90%
2007	Peru	94%	Argentina	−4%	98%
2008	Morocco	−11%	Pakistan	−74%	63%

Note: Price returns in US dollars.
Source: Thomson Datastream, MSCI Inc.[2] as of 12/31/2008.

Table 6.2   Best- and Worst-Performing Emerging
Market Sector by Year

Year	Best Sector	Max	Worst Sector	Min	Spread
1995	Tech	11.6%	Materials	−14.5%	26.1%
1996	Energy	29.8%	Tech	−15.3%	45.1%
1997	Energy	18.4%	Industrials	−41.0%	59.4%
1998	Tech	4.0%	Energy	−51.4%	55.5%
1999	Tech	138.6%	Industrials	28.1%	110.5%
2000	Health Care	1.4%	Tech	−44.7%	46.1%
2001	Energy	14.2%	Telecom	−18.2%	32.4%
2002	Materials	18.0%	Tech	−22.0%	40.0%
2003	Energy	84.7%	Consumer Staples	39.9%	44.8%
2004	Financials	39.5%	Health Care	7.7%	31.8%
2005	Energy	62.4%	Industrials	25.5%	36.9%
2006	Utilities	47.4%	Health Care	−8.6%	56.1%
2007	Industrials	69.6%	Tech	2.1%	67.5%
2008	Health Care	−17.4%	Industrials	−62.0%	44.6%

Source: Thomson Datastream, MSCI Inc.[3]

the best- and worst-performing countries tends to be substantial. In 2007, for instance, there was nearly a 100 percent spread between Peru (94 percent) and Argentina (−4 percent), even though they are neighbors in the same region and share some of the same drivers!

Second, country leadership changes often because drivers change. Russia is the only country to repeat as the best performer two years in a row (and that was only once, in 1996–1997), and countries have often moved from best to worst (and vice versa). The drivers behind Peru's outperformance in 2007 clearly didn't hold moving forward—the country fell 40 percent in 2008.[1]

A similar phenomenon exists across sectors. Table 6.2 shows the best- and worst-performing sectors in emerging markets and the spread each year since 1995 (unfortunately, sector data are limited going back in time). Spreads are generally narrower than countries where leadership repeats more often. But the difference is still substantial enough to greatly impact relative performance. Thus, success will be greatly determined by your ability to properly identify the countries and sectors most likely to outperform or underperform. This, in turn, rests on being able to correctly develop and analyze portfolio drivers.

THE PROPER PERSPECTIVE

To begin developing portfolio drivers, it's necessary to achieve proper context. As mentioned in Chapter 2, stock prices are ultimately a function of supply and demand. This is basic Economics 101, yet most investors fail to consider pricing mechanisms in this context. They're often distracted and overwhelmed by talking heads on television, "research reports" from brokerage firms, or even their next-door neighbor spouting any number of economic, technical, or crazy conspiracy theories. These may make for interesting storylines, but they aren't going to help you develop sound investing drivers. Rather, it all boils down to the mundane economic laws of supply and demand. To appropriately identify drivers, you must frame stocks in this context.

The supply of most goods can quickly change. For instance, most modern cars can be assembled in a day; Toyota can rapidly adjust the pace of manufacturing to account for changes in demand. Not so for securities. New stocks usually come to market via an initial public offering (IPO) or secondary offering. Just think how long these need to evolve and the amount of advance notice companies are required by law to give investors. Creating or destroying supply takes time and effort, allowing you to pretty much assume it's fixed in the short term. Stock prices 10 years from now will be determined more by what happens to supply in eight or nine years, not today.

Demand, on the other hand, can shift powerfully in the short term and is therefore more important in making a forecast for the here and now. Any number of daily, weekly, or monthly events can shift the demand for stocks—a management change, a quarter or two of bad economic data, and so on. The list is endless. But with quickness comes fickleness. Thus, you shouldn't try to forecast too far into the future because the winds of demand can shift quickly. Ever been asked where you see yourself in 10 years? While some may have an idea where they *want* to be, there's a good chance the end result will differ. Life is simply too uncertain to accurately predict that far ahead. Capital markets act similarly; we cannot possibly know where stocks will be 5 to 10 years from now. Anyone that tells you otherwise is telling you more about their overconfidence than their forecasting prowess.

Staying focused on the short term also means you should avoid putting too much weight in the big, secular trends so often cited as positives for emerging markets. As in, "China and India have an absolute mass of people bound to inextricably alter the face of such and such industry forever." Undoubtedly, you've heard this line of reasoning before, and for good reason—it makes intuitive sense and there is much truth to it. But it's a big, slow-moving thing and isn't likely to drive markets in a given year. Instead, you should focus on the incremental changes within the larger trend. You'll have more success at identifying the winners over a shorter period.

Successfully identifying drivers is also rarely achieved by following the herd—you need to see things others don't. Capital markets are highly effective discounters of all widely known information. Therefore, to add value, investors must identify information not widely known or interpret widely known information differently from other market participants. We aren't advocating betting the reverse of the consensus—what most people consider *contrarianism*. A contrarian is correct in thinking what everyone assumes will happen rarely does, but wrongly assumes the exact opposite will happen. If the consensus expects the markets to rise 10 percent next year, contrarians bet it will fall. But markets could just as easily be flat or up 20 percent or more. Surprises are what move markets, not the consensus. That's where you should mine for your portfolio drivers: Understand what is widely expected and decide how reality will under- or overshoot that expectation.

Last, if you expect what follows to provide a checklist for your next portfolio rebalance, you'll be sorely disappointed. Markets are constantly changing, meaning the evaluation of drivers and market conditions requires a dynamic approach. Success won't come from rote memorization of contributing factors and applying those indiscriminately going forward. Instead, you need a general framework—one flexible enough to account for a wide variety of market conditions and adjustable as appropriate.

IDENTIFYING PORTFOLIO DRIVERS

Identifying portfolio drivers begins with an analysis of three broad categories of factors that influence relative performance the most: *economics*, *politics*, and *sentiment*. These factors work across all categories of stocks, but the drivers within them will vary considerably depending on both place and time. Some are explicitly related to country decisions; others pertain more to sectors. But most are broad enough to have an impact on both, and investors should analyze each one with this in mind. Here, we detail many important factors across the three main categories of drivers, with key questions to ask as you go about the process.

Economic Drivers

Economic drivers are things related to the macroeconomic environment. This could include monetary policy, interest rates, lending activity, yield curve analysis, relative GDP growth analysis, and myriad others. What economic forces are likely to drive GDP growth throughout countries in the world? What is the outlook for interest rates and how would that impact sectors? What is the outlook for technology and infrastructure spending among countries?

Economic drivers pertain not only to the fundamental outlook of the economy (GDP growth, interest rates, inflation), but also to the stock market (valuations, M&A activity, share buybacks). As an investor, it's your job to identify these drivers and determine how they'll impact your overall portfolio and each of its segments.

Important economic drivers include:

- **Relative GDP growth**: Investors often wrongly assume strong absolute economic growth translates into stock market outperformance. Economic growth *is* a valid driver; it's just relative growth that matters. Ask yourself how fast a country is growing relative to its peers. How does it compare to recent history? Is growth accelerating or slowing? Does growth compare favorably to other countries with a similar economic structure (e.g., how does growth compare across countries reliant on exports)? How are the underlying sectors of the economy performing? Is domestic demand leading growth? Exports? Investment spending? Is the trend sustainable?

- **Monetary policy**: Monetary policy affects the economic environment through a number of channels—interest rates, liquidity, and inflationary expectations, to name a few. Some key questions to ask: Is the central bank raising or lowering interest rates? Do the various measures of money supply (M0, M1, M2, etc.) suggest the environment is tight or loose? Are banks lending and multiplying the money throughout the economy? Are reserve requirements changing?

- **Inflation**: High and wildly gyrating rates of inflation are generally bad for economic activity (see Chapter 3). Is inflation, as measured by the consumer price index (CPI), high or low? Trending downward or rising? Relatively stable or erratic? Are "core" measures of inflation—which exclude volatile energy and food prices—showing a different trend? What do other market indicators, such as inflation-protected securities or bond yields, say about inflation expectations? Are price changes different across industries? If so, which industries does this help or hurt?

- **Relative interest rates**: Domestically, interest rates primarily impact lending. Are interest rates low enough to encourage borrowing? How do they compare relative to historical standards? Is the central bank raising or lowering short-term rates? More broadly, interest rates also reflect the relative attractiveness of capital to foreigners, with higher rates increasing the likelihood of investor interest.

- **Yield curve**: Related to interest rates, the yield curve reflects the degree of banking profitability. Banks take deposits at short-term rates and lend at long-term rates. This spread is called the *net interest margin* (NIM). When it's positive—long rates above short rates, or an upward-sloping yield curve—banks are incentivized to lend, a good thing for overall economic and investment activity.

- **Currency strength**: Emerging market currencies are volatile and prone to big swings, making currency strength a powerful driver. Ask yourself if the currency prone to speculation. Has it been devalued in the past? How are political and social events affecting sentiment? What's driving most recent performance? Interest rate or growth differentials? Capital flows? Inflation expectations? Currency strength also has different impacts on different industries. For example, a weak currency helps exporters by making their goods cheaper in foreign markets.

Primary Influences of Currency Supply and Demand

Currencies derive their relative value the same way as other assets—by supply and demand. Supply is determined solely by the issuing central bank; it has a monopoly on the creation or destruction of its own currency. Currency demand, however, is determined by a wide variety of factors. Principal among them is the amount of economic activity being conducted, its role as a store of value, and the level of relative interest rates. Here are some of the primary influences of currency supply and demand:

SHORT RUN (DAYS, WEEKS, AND MONTHS)

- *Jawboning*: When a senior government or central bank official speaks favorably or unfavorably about a currency, it can affect sentiment and shift demand. This effect can last a matter of minutes to a few weeks.
- *Central bank open market operations*: When a central bank buys one currency in exchange for another. This is often fleeting, as no central bank; has a big enough balance sheet to overwhelm other factors for long.
- *Speculators*: When a private economic agent buys or sells a currency in hopes of anticipating others will do the same. In isolation, speculators have a lesser effect than central bank operations due to smaller balance sheets. But, in a synchronized

fashion, they can have a magnified impact. Many attribute the contagion following the Asian Financial Crisis to speculators (see Chapter 2).

INTERMEDIATE RUN (MONTHS TO A YEAR)

- *Interest rate differentials*: Demand for financial assets is attracted to higher yielding assets and away from lower yielding ones. When one country's interest rates are higher than another, the demand for that country's currency typically rises.
- *Economic growth rate differentials*: When one country grows faster than another, the demand for its currency increases because of more transactions in that currency and the belief assets there will have a higher return on investment.
- *Non-discretionary central bank operations*: When a country pegs its currency to another (e.g., Singapore dollar to the US dollar), the country must buy and sell currency to maintain the peg.

LONG RUN (YEARS)

- *Excess money supply growth differentials (inflation rate differentials)*: When a central bank excessively creates money relative to real economic growth, the excess supply depresses the price of the currency and increases inflation. More money for the same amount of assets decreases the currency's store of value.

- **Debt levels**: As evidenced by its turbulent history, debt levels can vary dramatically in emerging markets, often to negative effect. Remember, debt levels are relative—some debt is often a good thing—and distinguish between private and public debt. Do households and business have access to credit? Is the debt service burden acceptable (i.e., are interest rates reasonable or punitive)? What currency is the debt denominated in? Is debt finding its way into productive hands?
- **M&A, issuance, and repurchase activity**: These actions fundamentally shape the supply of securities. M&A and repurchase activity generally *reduce* supply by lowering the total shares outstanding. Thus, increased M&A and repurchase activity is good for markets. Equity issuance, however, is the exact opposite since it *increases* the available supply. Are there any granular trends within sectors (e.g., are utilities companies consolidating)?

New issuance can also be positive for more underdeveloped markets since it increases market depth.

- **Infrastructure spending**: Infrastructure refers to basic physical systems like communication, transportation, or electricity networks. Spending on new infrastructure increases efficiency and productivity and can be broadly stimulative to the economy. How much of a government's budget is going to new infrastructure? In what segment of the economy is that money being spent? Is private spending occurring (often at the company level)? Do any particular sectors stand to benefit, either as the recipient of such spending or the actual construction?

Political Drivers

Political drivers can be country-specific, pertain to regions (Asia, Latin America), or affect interaction between countries or regions (such as trade policies). These drivers are more concerned with categories such as taxation, government stability, fiscal policy, and political turnover. Which countries are experiencing a change in government that could have a meaningful impact on their economies? Which sectors could be at risk from new taxation or legislation? Which countries are undergoing pro-growth reforms?

Political drivers will help determine the relative attractiveness of market segments and countries. Be warned, however: Most investors suffer from "home country bias," where they ascribe too much emphasis on the politics of their own country. Always keep in mind it's a big, interconnected world, and geopolitical developments everywhere can have implications.

Political drivers also tend to be exaggerated in emerging markets. Big changes often occur rapidly; even entire governments can be overthrown in days. Thailand, for example, has witnessed 10 coup d'états since 1971.[4] Given the potential for surprise, politics is an especially powerful driver in emerging markets. Some of the most important aspects:

- **Government stability**: In the developed world, we often take government stability for granted, but it's often a major concern

in emerging markets. Fractured party systems can be destabilized by myriad competing interests, and shaky coalitions may
perpetuate weak governance and slow progress on reform. Other
countries have the exact opposite problem, either as a de facto
one-party state (e.g., South Africa) or an authoritarian regime
(e.g., China) that won't easily budge.

- **Taxation**: Are tax rates low enough to incentivize economic
  growth? Do any industries receive special tax breaks? How do the
  overall levels of taxation compare to other countries? Is compliance simple or complicated? Are tax receipts stronger or weaker
  than expected (a sign of economic activity)? What are the tax
  rates by industry? Do any receive tax breaks? Face tariffs in other
  countries?
- **Trade/Capital barriers**: Barriers like a closed capital account
  or trade restrictions are impediments to the free flow of capital
  and bad for markets. Does the country have an open or closed
  capital account? Has it entered into any free trade agreements?
  How are relationships with its neighbors? Do tariffs or subsidies
  distort the competitive attributes of any industries?
- **Fiscal policy**: Analyze the government's broader fiscal policy. What
  segment of society is it catered to? Business? A particular economic
  sector? The poor? Does it promote redistributive measures (a negative)? Is the government spending wisely? Who are the potential
  winners and losers of any spending programs? How is spending
  being financed? With growth? Higher taxes? External debt?
- **Political turnover**: Generally, capital markets fear the uncertainty created by political change and abhor politicians artificially
  determining winners and losers. Know when a country has federal, state, or local elections scheduled and the ideological beliefs
  of the primary political parties. Analyze their platforms leading
  up to the election. Will they maintain the status quo? Are they
  generally good for business? Do any sectors stand to benefit or
  suffer from the change? Do they promote structural reform?
- **Property rights**: Property rights are fundamental to well-
  functioning capital markets. Can citizens freely buy and sell

property and expect to retain it without worry of seizure? How ingrained are legal and judicial institutions? Is there a distinct separation of powers? Checks and balances? If property rights exist, how well are they enforced? Do any sectors receive special treatment from the government?

- **Protectionism**: *Protectionism* refers broadly to government actions restricting the free flow of trade. This includes tariffs, taxes, quotas, or other restrictive actions. Such policies are often used to protect a vulnerable domestic industry from foreign competition. And since emerging markets represent a threat as low-cost producers, protectionist measures are often enacted with them in mind. Since protectionism artificially distorts natural market mechanizations, it is viewed negatively by investors.

- **Corruption**: Corruption is commonplace in emerging markets, but its impact as a driver is less straightforward. The actual act invariably creates inefficiencies as consumers and businesses go about their day-to-day affairs. But it is tough to measure, so focus on the broader picture. Does corruption threaten progress on reform? Endanger government stability? Decrease the transparency of particular industries?

- **Privatization**: The state often plays a large role in emerging market countries. As a more efficient allocator of capital, private enterprise is generally preferred to government control. To what extent is the government selling state assets to the private sector? What sectors are affected? After privatization, does the state maintain any involvement? Are privatized industries truly free and unrestricted?

- **Structural reform**: Structural reform refers broadly to change in a country's economic or political framework that increases efficiency or allows capital markets to operate more freely. This may include simplifying the tax code to reduce the cost of compliance or change in financial regulation to allow banks to more freely lend. What reform, if any, is the existing government promoting? Have they successfully made progress? Are there any political impediments, such as a lack of support from the legislature?

- **Social stability**: Social stability is often weaker in emerging markets due to starker demographic diversity. Income, race, and religion, for example, can all substantially influence markets. Are there competing racial or religious groups within a country? What is the general level of income inequality across demographic groups? Are any of these differences institutionalized, like South Africa's Black Economic Empowerment (BEE) (see Chapter 4)?
- **General levels of freedom**: The level of economic, political, and social freedom in emerging markets also has a bearing on performance. The Heritage Foundation publishes the Index of Economic Freedom, which scores the freedom levels of 183 countries around the world across various factors (www.heritage.org/Index/Default.aspx). The higher a country ranks on the scale, the "freer" it is. All else being equal, a freer country is a good thing for investors. The 2009 rankings illustrate the clear distinction between emerging and developed markets: The UK ranks 10th, while Russia ranks 146th. This is an imperfect measurement, but telling nonetheless.

Sentiment Drivers

Sentiment drivers attempt to measure consensus thinking about investment categories. In the quest to know something others don't or interpret widely held information differently, sentiment drivers are vital inputs—they reflect expectations and what the market is discounting. Surprises move markets, so use these drivers to help you find areas where sentiment is different than reality. For example, let's say you observe most investors currently expect a recession in the next year. But you disagree and believe GDP growth will be strong. This presents an excellent opportunity for excess returns. You can load up on stocks that will benefit from an economic boom and watch your portfolio rise as the rest of the market realizes it later and prices in the result.

Since the market is a discounter of all known information, it's important to try and identify what the market is pricing in. Looking forward, which sectors are investors most bullish about and why? What countries or sectors are widely discussed in the media? What market segments have been bid up recently based on something other than fundamentals? If the market's perception is different than fundamentals in the short term, stocks will eventually correct themselves to reflect reality in the long term. Key sentiment drivers include:

- **Mutual fund/portfolio flows**: Mutual fund and portfolio flows capture investor demand for the securities of a particular country or asset class. Is money flowing into or out of a country or sector? How much and how fast? Investors are fickle, so these flows can be transient and short term. And, too often, this money flows toward the flavor of the month, so be wary of chasing heat.
- **Foreign investment**: Beyond mutual fund and portfolio flows, there is another measure of investment demand: foreign direct investment (FDI). FDI consists of more tangible investments than portfolio flows, such as a new factory or bridge. Because they often represent longer-term investments, these flows are scrutinized by investors. Keep an eye out for countries (or sectors) both *giving* and *receiving* this type of investment.
- **Media coverage**: Media coverage is a powerful qualitative measure of sentiment. What is the tone of the media coverage for a country? Are journalists writing favorably about its economic, political, or social environment? Or is negative news pervasive? Do "local" opinion sources differ from "foreign" sources?
- **Risk aversion:** General levels of risk aversion can drive performance of a particular country or sector. For example, if risk aversion increases, investors may sell out of smaller, riskier countries (like Thailand or Argentina) or sectors sensitive to the business cycle (like Industrials).
- **Consumer confidence**: The most widely quoted measure of investor sentiment. It has some relevance as a coincidental indicator, meaning it tells you how people feel right now. But because it isn't telling you anything about what people will feel going forward, the power of these figures is often overstated. Collection methods can also be spotty so be sure to evaluate how the data are calculated before putting too much stock in what they say.

- **Professional investor forecasts**: Taken together, professional forecasters represent a good proxy for consensus expectations. If every major forecaster is bullish on a country, seriously analyze whether expectations have gone too far. Do the economic and political drivers warrant such optimism? Is another country with positive drivers ignored because of the myopic focus on one country?
- **Momentum cycle analysis**: Stock market momentum refers to the rate of acceleration of a category of stocks or security's price. Is a country or sector continuously moving downward? This may suggest investors have become overly pessimistic. The opposite is also true.

TRANSLATING DRIVERS INTO PORTFOLIO ALLOCATION DECISIONS

Once you've completed a thorough analysis of potential economic, political, and sentiment drivers, you need to translate what you've found into portfolio allocation decisions.

Remember that capital markets are highly effective discounters of all widely known information. Therefore, you're looking for drivers not widely appreciated or those misinterpreted by the market. Are any of your drivers showing "extreme" readings? Are there any outliers? These are the areas that should generally drive your major allocation decisions. For example, maybe your analysis reveals that structural reform in South Korea has given the shipbuilding industry easier access to cheaper imported steel. Shipbuilders rallied considerably after the announcement, but steelmakers have barely budged—this may be a category of stocks worth further analysis.

Your degree of confidence in the underlying drivers will determine the weighting difference relative to the benchmark. No investment is without risk, and recognition of risk is just as important as identifying potential positives. Ideally, you're looking for a few high-conviction areas to place your largest over- and underweights. Areas you have less confidence in can be neutral weights or minor over- and underweights.

Sometimes, allocation decisions are predicated on exclusionary management. That is, maybe you can only confidently determine areas to underweight. In this case, you might overweight the remaining categories because they should have a higher expected return. To better give you a feel for how an evaluation of portfolio drivers works in practice, here's an example featuring Brazil.

AN ILLUSTRATION IN ANALYZING PORTFOLIO DRIVERS—BRAZIL DURING THE 2003–2007 BULL MARKET

At the end of 2002, Brazil hardly looked like a contender for country leadership. Economic growth seemed pedestrian compared to the blistering figures reported in other emerging markets like China and India, with GDP rising a mere 1.3 percent in 2001.[5] Confidence remained shaken following another currency devaluation in 1999— the fifth in less than 10 years. And a noted populist threatened to end a growing trend of positive political reform. The country's weak relative market performance reflected the pervading uncertainty—Brazil fell an annualized 20 percent from 2000 through 2002, compared to a decline of 14 percent for the MSCI Emerging Markets Index.[6]

In 2003, global equities entered a five-year bull market that saw the MSCI World Index return an average annualized 18 percent. Emerging markets performed even better, rising 37 percent a year over the same period. But Brazil blew away nearly every other country in the world, posting a 65 percent annualized return. What drove such a dramatic reversal? In this section, we evaluate the political, economic, and sentiment drivers behind Brazil's stunning outperformance.

Set the Stage

In 2002, Brazil prepared for a new president—the second term of President Fernando Cardoso's administration was coming to an end. Elections are one of the most important political drivers, as they represent the greatest probability of change. As such, investors tend to view them cautiously, and this one was no different.

The outgoing president, Fernando Cardoso, was a firm proponent of fiscal responsibility. As finance minister, he helped lead the country out from hyperinflation with his "Real Plan" in 1994.[7] In his second term, Cardoso passed several landmark laws, including the Fiscal Responsibility Law in 2000, which imposed greater controls on government spending. Given Brazil's historical lack of fiscal discipline, this was a welcome change.

Cardoso also introduced additional sound reform. Presidential Decree 3088, issued in January 1999, established inflation targeting as the official monetary regime for the Brazilian central bank. Brazil's long history of hyperinflation wreaked havoc on economic and financial stability; the sheer scale of price changes and its violently unpredictable nature continuously frightened away investors. While the Real Plan successfully brought inflation down from the heady levels of previous administrations, Cardoso's decision to institute inflation targeting helped keep it under control. These reforms represented positive political drivers—much rested on their continuation in the next administration.

Inflation Targeting

With inflation targeting, the central bank makes public a "target" inflation rate and attempts to guide actual inflation to it with monetary policy tools like interest rate changes. Inflation targeting is largely a credibility exercise—the central bank is openly communicating with the market in an attempt to demonstrate inflation remains predictable and in control. Many countries have official inflation-targeting regimes, like the UK, Canada, and Australia.

But Cardoso's successor potentially threatened this progress. A former metalworker and union leader, Luiz Inacio Lula da Silva (known commonly as Lula) gained popularity by leading strikes against the Brazilian military dictatorships of the 1970s and 1980s. He also helped found the Worker's Party, the dominant left-wing party of Brazilian politics.

Given his background and Brazil's history of populist-leaning leaders, Lula frightened investors. He had a history of fiery anti-capitalist rhetoric, promoting such causes as intentional debt default and the renationalization of state-owned enterprises. At best, investors feared he would ditch the market-friendly policies introduced under Cardoso's regime. At worst, he represented a return to the country's populist ways. Investors held their collective breaths and the uncertainty weighed on markets—Brazilian stocks sold off in the run-up to elections. This was a political driver at work.

Investors were also suspicious of the economy. Crises in Argentina and Uruguay erupted into fears of contagion across the region. Even though Brazil was financially separated from these trouble spots, it was still viewed by investors as Latin American. Contagion represents both a sentiment and an economic driver. It is based mostly on fear (sentiment) but is also in response to the visible deterioration of some corner of the market (economic). In either case, traders thrashed the Brazilian real to historic lows, interest rates and inflation spiked, and major credit rating agencies began questioning the country's ability to service its $250 billion in debt.[8] Taking stock at the end of 2002, uncertainty remained high. Investors were unsure what elections might bring, and the economic outlook appeared murky.

Analyze the Current Environment and Outlook

Lula took office in 2003 and quickly assuaged investors' fears. Upon assuming office, the 35th president of Brazil hardly resembled the leader suggested by his past. He toned down his populist rhetoric and adopted many of Cardoso's key policies on fiscal responsibility and inflation targeting.

The fear of change soon morphed into optimism of further change. Lula didn't just keep the market-friendly policies of his predecessor, he built on them. For example, the pension system was bloated from the populist handouts of previous administrations—pensions cost the government nearly $20 billion, or 4 percent of GDP at the time.[9] One of Lula's first actions as president involved reforming this system. He passed laws limiting the size of public-sector pensions and made them taxable. These moves were very unpopular; Brazil's politicians had long cemented their hold on power through the support of the masses. But markets welcomed the structural reform. They represented a break from Brazil's damaging populist past.

But the administration wasn't done yet. Brazilian consumers and businesses had long starved for credit. Not only were interest rates prohibitively high, but structural inefficiencies deterred banks from lending more. For example, Brazilian reserve-to-deposit requirements were among the highest in the world. This manifested itself in a generally low level of credit across the economy, even by emerging market standards. Credit availability is a crucial variable to the efficient functioning of markets, a key economic driver.

Lula focused on structural reforms to increase the overall availability of credit. A series of measures, such as changes to bankruptcy law and the framework for securitization, coaxed banks to take more risk and increase lending. With interest rates and inflation already heading downward, banks were now more apt to extend loans after reform. And lend they did. Bank lending rose from 25 percent of GDP in 2003 to just over 40 percent in 2008. This had clear positive economic ramifications: During this period, capital goods production consistently grew over 20 percent year-over-year, and retail sales, which were declining in 2003, began to grow at double-digit rates.[10] In this case, positive political drivers (structural reform) helped shape economic drivers (increased lending).

Continued reform boosted investor confidence and led to other enticing economic drivers. Inflation, long the country's nemesis, remained steady and predictable, encouraging investment, consumption, and ultimately higher economic growth (see Figure 6.1). Capital goods production consistently grew over 20 percent year-over-year, and retail sales, which were *declining* in 2003, began to grow at double-digit rates. Not surprisingly, Brazilian Financials performed extremely well due to the windfall of credit reform, returning 69 percent annualized from 2003 to 2007.[11]

In addition to positive domestic drivers, there were larger, more powerful trends brewing outside Brazil's borders. In the developed world, we often take for granted the electricity lighting our homes, the roads facilitating easy transport, or the clean water systems providing one of our most basic human needs. But this infrastructure is

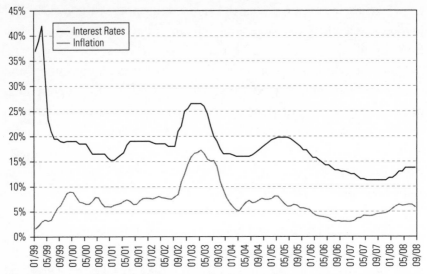

Figure 6.1 Brazil Inflation and Interest Rates Since Inflation Targeting
Source: Thomson Datastream.

generally inferior or non-existent in emerging markets. Rapid economic growth and industrialization in recent years only exacerbated the strain on existing resources.

In response, governments deployed enormous amounts of capital to upgrade the emerging world at the turn of the twenty-first century. At the same time, cracks began to form in the developed world, much of which was industrialized 100 years ago. Its infrastructure began to deteriorate and, in some cases, fail completely. The developed world needed a refresh. Together, these trends unleashed an investment boom seen only a few times in history (an economic driver). And because of its resource-heavy market composition, Brazil was one of its biggest beneficiaries.

Infrastructure requires two key inputs—raw materials and energy. You can't build a skyscraper without steel beams or a road without concrete, and the surge in infrastructure spending dramatically increased demand for basic materials. From 1980 to 2000, global crude steel production, a metal required for manufacturing and construction, grew 18 percent. In the seven years from 2000 to 2006, however, production increased 58 percent.[12] Increased demand for

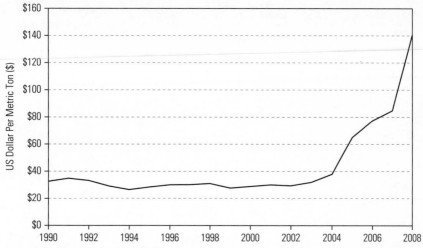

Figure 6.2   Iron Ore Benchmark Prices
Source: International Monetary Fund.

steel in turn led to demand for iron ore, its main ingredient (see Figure 6.2). In addition, the wave of industrialization dramatically increased demand for oil and its derivatives, pushing up oil prices more than five-fold.[13]

This was a powerful economic driver for Brazil, as the country was the world's second-largest producer of iron ore and also home to a large energy sector.[14] Together, the Energy and Materials sectors account for nearly 50 percent of the country's weight. Both clearly benefited from the global thirst for commodities, returning an annualized 73 percent and 82 percent from 2003 to 2007, respectively (see Table 6.3).

The commodities boom presents a few key takeaways. First, investors cannot ignore the structural composition of each country's market. One of the first steps to evaluating a country should be an understanding of its sector composition. Here, recognition of the larger infrastructure theme would have likely led you to Brazilian Materials and Energy regardless of your view on the country. Second, don't forget to think globally. In today's globalized world, not every reason for a country's relative market performance lays within its borders. A broader global trend can be just as impactful to a country if it provides a key input or is in some way connected.

Table 6.3   MSCI Brazil as of December 31, 2007

Sector	Weight	2003–2007 Annualized Return
Materials	25.0%	73.1%
Energy	23.2%	81.5%
Financials	14.5%	69.2%
Telecommunication Services	14.1%	33.3%
Consumer Staples	12.3%	43.4%
Utilities	7.0%	51.1%
Industrials	3.3%	34.4%
Consumer Discretionary	0.5%	34.2%
Health Care	0.0%	N/A
Information Technology	0.0%	N/A

Source: MSCI, Inc.,[15] Thomson Datastream.

Acknowledge and Evaluate Risks

No evaluation of portfolio drivers is complete without an in-depth analysis of risk. An underappreciated negative can sometimes outweigh an otherwise rosy outlook. Investors should therefore spend just as much time evaluating what could go wrong as what may go right.

And despite the ongoing positive developments, risks remained. Economically, Brazil as a country remained sensitive to market turbulence due to its reliance on foreign capital. Red tape still entangled businesses, fostering inefficiencies. And although interest rates were substantially lower than historical levels, they remained high on an absolute basis.

Politically, a series of scandals plagued much of Lula's first term and threatened progress on reform. Corruption is commonplace in emerging markets due to weak institutions and often poorly developed legal and regulatory frameworks. Lula was also going against the weight of historical trends; it takes a strong politician to consistently challenge the status quo. At any given point in time, Brazil's fragmented political process threatened to undo the progress made.

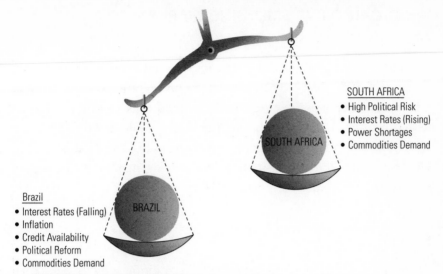

Figure 6.3   Weighing Portfolio Drivers

How Did It Stack Up?

The evaluation of portfolio drivers doesn't occur in a vacuum. In this case, a similar analysis of other countries in the benchmark would need to be conducted before determining the appropriate allocation to Brazil. After you've gone through the relevant markets, stack up countries (or sectors) relative to each other. Clearly, there were a number of positive drivers in Brazil. But how did they stack up against other emerging markets? We like to think of this process like a scale, with the heavier category represented as an overweight. Put one country (or sector) on each side. Which side would weigh more? By how much?

Figure 6.3 illustrates a very simple example of this idea, comparing Brazil to South Africa in the early 2000s. Like Brazil, South Africa also benefited from increased commodities demand because of its vast mineral resources. But while interest rates and inflation were falling in Brazil, they were rising in South Africa. And the political environment in South Africa was fraught with risk. Therefore, an overweight to Brazil relative to South Africa was justified. Utilizing this approach with each segment will help guide you in determining what areas of the market to over- and underweight.

WHAT CAN DRIVE EMERGING MARKETS AS A CATEGORY

Despite consisting of 24 different countries, each driven by a unique confluence of factors, broader asset class considerations can sometimes take precedence depending on market conditions. While the framework introduced earlier in the chapter is applicable here as well, there are several important factors worth further discussion. In this section, we discuss the factors that may drive emerging markets as a category to perform differently than developed markets.

Economic Growth

Emerging markets tend to have higher economic growth rates than developed markets. This is part of their allure to investors. But does stronger economic growth translate into stock outperformance?

The evidence suggests so—at least through its relatively short history. Using the 24 official countries in emerging markets today, the average annual GDP growth for the category since 1988 is 4.3 percent. The same number for developed markets is 2.8 percent.[16] Stock market performance over the same period is also in emerging markets' favor, with the MSCI Emerging Market Index returning an annualized average 11.4 percent versus 6.2 percent for the MSCI World Index.[17]

Taken at face value, these data suggest holding a constant overweight to emerging markets. After all, they offer stronger economic growth *and* higher stock market returns. However, this is dangerous logic in the short term. No category of stocks outperforms at all times, and emerging markets stocks are often subject to large swings in performance. In any given year, such a belief can lead to disappointing and unexpected negative returns. For example, the MSCI Emerging Markets Index *fell* an average annualized 9 percent from 1994 through 1998, while the MSCI World Index *rose* 16.2 percent a year over the same period.[18]

In addition, much of emerging markets' outperformance in the past two decades represents their arrival on the world stage. Growth was disproportionate in this beginning stage and, as it invariably slows, emerging markets may begin to perform more like their developed market peers over time. In the very long term, most equity indexes finish with roughly the same return.

Upon closer inspection, the connection between economic growth and stock market performance appears less straightforward. At the country level, for instance, there is little relationship between the two. In Chapter 2, we told the story of China's vicious 2001 to 2005 bear market, a time when the Chinese economy averaged double-digit growth. Investors indiscriminately following the country with the best economic growth would have seen their portfolio wilt. To be sure, the two are not mutually exclusive—a strong economy can certainly be *one* driver behind market outperformance. But solely using economic growth as a guide for portfolio allocation may just as often lead to trouble.

A better approach is to take a step back and consider emerging markets' role in the global economy. Economic development happens in several stages. Most societies are agrarian to start, largely for means of self-sustenance. Eventually, productivity increases enough for a society to specialize and trade for goods it has neither the skills nor the resources to produce. Over time, the country moves up the value-chain, developing a manufacturing base to produce more sophisticated goods.

The Value Chain

Imagine the production of a good—say, the corn flakes you ate this morning for breakfast. At the most basic level, corn flakes are corn; thus, their production begins with the corn farmer planting seed. Following that, a spate of other economic players take their turn in the production process: Fertilizer firms increase the corn crop's yield; tractor manufacturers foster more efficient harvests; trucking firms haul the crop to cereal manufacturers; marketing companies brand and sell; and so on until the box of cereal ends up in consumers' hands. Each step along the way represents a unique position on the *value-chain*: a chain of activities that at each point adds value to a product. Generally, initial stages of the value-chain are low-cost and low-technology like the farmer taking plow to soil. As production moves up the chain, activity becomes increasingly sophisticated, requiring additional knowledge, training, cost, and technology like the marketing company designing the cereal box to best appeal to its target audience.

This happened in the developed world at various stages throughout the eighteenth and nineteenth centuries—think of the US' humble progression from Pilgrim farmers to railroad magnates. The continuous fight for progress rarely slows, and many societies move further toward high-margin and knowledge-based services, such as banking or engineering.

Emerging markets are predominantly in the early stages of this development cycle. While many still cling to their agricultural past, most have recently industrialized, replacing the developed world as the source for lower-end manufacturing. This means emerging markets represent the beginning phases of the global economic production cycle and tend to be more sensitive to expectations of world economic growth.

The lesson for investors: Emerging markets tend to perform well when expectations of global economic growth are strong and underperform during downturns. So your expectations for emerging markets as a category should invariably include some evaluation of global growth expectations.

How does an investor possibly begin to evaluate something so broad? First, consider (though not necessarily heed) the consensus. Various organizations, such as the IMF and big brokerage houses, publish growth expectations. Get a feel for what they're saying and why. Ask yourself if you agree and why, and then brainstorm alternative scenarios. What do *you* think would surprise markets or cause an economy to deviate from the consensus? Feel free to be as creative as you like. Think aliens might invade Russia? Go ahead and jot it down.

Once you've thoroughly exhausted every conceivable option, go back and assign a probability to each of your scenarios. Don't feel pressured to be overly precise. Remember, investing isn't a certainties business—you're simply trying to objectively evaluate a range of possibilities. Do this often enough, and you'll notice your conclusions differ in some ways from the consensus. Even if it's a subtle difference, it can have important allocation implications. Imagine the consensus believes the global economy will grow like gangbusters, but you see it growing positively at an average pace. In this case, maybe you underweight emerging markets slightly because you believe there is a greater probability of downside surprise.

Risk Environment

Beyond economic growth, the overall risk environment is another important driver for the emerging markets. Investors perceive emerging markets to be risky investments. This is warranted—returns are volatile and the political, economic, and social environments are often chaotic. Because of this added risk perception, emerging markets tend

Beta Coeffecient

The *beta coefficient* (or *beta*) describes how an investment behaves relative to the market as a whole. A stock that performs exactly in line with the chosen market would have a beta of 1. The higher the number, the riskier the asset. For example, if a stock's beta is 1.5, it's theoretically 50 percent more volatile than the market. In finance theory, beta represents the part of portfolio return that cannot be diversified away, or the *systematic* risk.

to perform in line with the overall risk environment—when investors are fearful, emerging markets underperform; when optimistic, they outperform. In other words, emerging markets act like high beta plays on global equities.

To see this at work, consider a recent example: The global bear market beginning November 2007. A full explanation of the events surrounding this period is beyond the scope of this book, but, broadly, the crisis began in the developed markets and emerging markets played little to no part. Unfortunately, that doesn't mean they were left unscathed—investors pummeled the category in tandem with developed markets from the start. This was an interesting phenomenon at the time, defying emerging markets' historic role as riskier, higher-beta plays on global equities (one would expect emerging markets to decline *more*). But strong fundamentals justified their relative resiliency: Economic growth remained robust, government officials built up war chests of foreign currency reserves in the preceding years, and monetary and fiscal policy was increasingly stimulative.

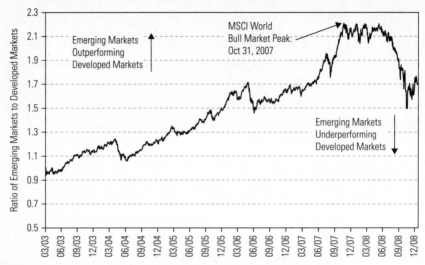

Figure 6.4   Emerging Market Relative Performance
Source: Thomson Datastream, MSCI Inc.[19]

Yet, as economic data from developed markets continued to darken, investors' overall perception of risk continued to follow suit. Even though fundamentals for many emerging market countries and securities remained solid, the overall risk environment deteriorated, and the category paid the price simply for what they generally were: risky assets. Figure 6.4 shows the marked turn in emerging markets' relative performance to developed markets at the beginning of 2008. Note how emerging markets traded sideways relative to developed markets at the start of the bear market (i.e., both categories were declining at roughly the same rate). By May 2008, emerging markets began to underperform considerably.

A related concept introduced in earlier chapters is worth reiterating. *Contagion* describes the transmission of a crisis across many countries, including those with no apparent fundamental link to its cause. Emerging markets are especially vulnerable to this behavior. As such, negative events in only a small handful of countries can weigh on the entire asset class.

Table 6.4   Emerging and Developed Market Sector Weights

Sector	Emerging Markets	Developed Markets	Difference
Telecommunication Services	13.6%	5.3%	8.4%
Materials	12.8%	5.8%	6.9%
Financials	22.8%	18.6%	4.2%
Energy	14.9%	11.6%	3.2%
Information Technology	10.8%	10.2%	0.6%
Utilities	4.0%	5.7%	−1.7%
Industrials	7.7%	10.9%	−3.2%
Consumer Discretionary	4.8%	8.9%	−4.1%
Consumer Staples	5.8%	11.1%	−5.3%
Health Care	2.9%	11.9%	−9.0%

Source: Thomson Datastream, MSCI Inc.[20] as of 12/31/2008.

Structural Differences

Structural differences also drive performance for the emerging markets category. Table 6.4 illustrates the differences in sector weights between the developed and emerging markets. Aside from Information Technology, they are notably different.

Clearly, if you expected Health Care to lead the market in the period ahead, you'd also expect emerging markets to underperform. Likewise, if you were particularly bullish on global Telecommunication Services, you would expect emerging markets to outperform. Emerging markets are also more associated with commodities, as they have over 10 percent more weight devoted to the Energy and Materials sectors. If you are interested in learning about the drivers behind individual sectors, see the *Fisher Investments On* series.

Availability of Securities

In its formative years in the late 1980s and early 1990s, emerging markets was an esoteric asset class. A small group of early adopters sought exposure to an untapped segment of the equity universe and the low correlations and diversification that came with it. This is less true today. Emerging markets are increasingly integrated into the global economy and beginning to converge with developed markets. A dedicated allocation to emerging markets has become increasingly necessary for proper international equity exposure.

While the diversification benefits of emerging markets have decreased, the increased demand has made the asset class more accessible to investors. The introduction of American Depositary Receipts (ADRs) gave the average US investor access to securities previously only available to institutional investors with contacts in local markets. More recently, the increasing availability of exchange-traded funds (ETFs) has given retail investors the ability to acquire exposure to the entire category with one security. Financial innovation will surely persist, and the further lowering of barriers to investment will continue to contribute to emerging market demand relative to other categories.

A Confluence of Country Factors

Often, a trend across several countries can drive performance for the broader category. In the early 2000s, for instance, emerging markets on balance enacted pro-growth reforms and reduced tax burdens. In 2002, South Korea offered tax breaks and other incentives to investors in an effort to attract capital—companies investing more than $50 million in the country received exemptions from corporate and income taxes for an extended period.[21] Many other countries introduced similar investor-friendly measures, and, taken together, this trend represented a driver for the category as a whole.

GETTING INFORMATION TO DEVELOP DRIVERS

How do you get the information to conduct such an analysis? Investors often ask how they can possibly identify drivers without visiting a country, kicking the tires with management at a company's headquarters, or speaking the local language. The logic goes that the information disadvantage to doing none of these is so great that you're bound to miss something important, with your portfolio suffering as a result. Twenty years ago, there was some truth to this. But the world today is a vastly different place—most of the data you need to successfully invest in emerging markets rest right at your fingertips. You just need a computer and an Internet connection.

True, there are a limited number of hours in a day, and the average investor isn't working full time on his portfolio. However, the time you do have available—whatever amount that may be—should be spent on information gathering and analysis. That's how you generate actionable portfolio drivers. Warren Buffet was once asked how he got his investment ideas. His response: "I just read. I read all day."[22] We wholeheartedly agree.

Government Sources

Most economic data come from government sources and are often publicly available for free on the Internet. These websites offer information from interest rates to banking statistics to gross domestic product figures. Because not every organization produces the same set of figures across all countries, you may have to do a little bit of digging. For instance, Malaysia's inflation rate comes from the Department of Statistics Malaysia (www.statistics.gov.my/eng/), while Mexico's inflation rate is tracked by the country's central bank, Banco de Mexico (www.banxico.org.mx/sitioIngles/index.html).

If you don't know which government agency produces the data, look for a press release or newswire story on the subject. Most articles cite what source the data came from, as in "Mexico's consumer prices rose in February, according to the central bank," or something similar. Data can often be easily downloaded too, allowing you to track them over time or plot them out on a graph. And no need to fret language barriers—virtually every website these days offers an English-language version.

Third-Party Organizations

Data don't just come directly from the government. There are myriad third-party sources that either compile their own data or reinterpret figures from national sources. Two great resources, which are used extensively throughout this book, are the International Monetary Fund (IMF) and World Bank. The data may not be as timely as some of the figures offered by the government, but they can be invaluable when evaluating history or attempting to quickly glean high-level trends.

The IMF's World Economic Outlook Database (www.imf.org/external/data.htm), updated a few times a year, offers annual data on important figures, such as inflation, gross domestic product, and the current account balance. The World Bank complements these data with other statistics such as external debt and population growth (www.worldbank.org, see "Key Development Data & Statistics"). In addition to hard data, these sources also offer topical research papers and in-depth studies for those particularly inclined to get their hands dirty.

Company Filings

We'll touch on this a bit more in Chapter 7 when discussing security analysis, but a company's filings can also offer insight into a country's investment environment. Unfortunately, reporting standards are quite a bit more lax in emerging markets compared to the developed world. But many emerging market companies are increasingly becoming big, global players with secondary listings or ADRs on developed market exchanges, subjecting them to the higher regulatory and reporting standards of developed markets.

News Sources

Staying on top of day-to-day news is critical to the proper monitoring and development of portfolio drivers. If you don't pay attention to what's going on in the world, you can't possibly know if your drivers remain valid and risk new drivers passing by unnoticed.

Luckily, remaining informed is easier than ever before—there are almost too many choices. We suggest spreading your time across several different news sources to get different points of view. For general financial developments, a major daily such as the *Wall Street Journal* or *Financial Times* is highly recommended. Longer-dated periodicals such as the *Economist* or *BusinessWeek* are also worth occasional perusal. A variety of other sources provide a mix of commentary and just-the-facts reporting, such as Bloomberg.com, Reuters, BBC (British Broadcasting Company), and the like. And most emerging countries have a major daily rag in English that can offer a unique perspective, such as South Africa's *Mail & Guardian* or China's *China Daily*. Read through as many different sites as you can until you get a feel for the ones that offer the best content for your purposes. And change it up! Too many investors become habituated to the same columnists and editors; your job as an investor is to ascertain the right information and what the consensus believes.

Can You Trust It?

A common concern when investing in emerging markets is the credibility of published information. Because of weaker reporting standards and lower levels of ethical conduct, the data from emerging market nations often need to be taken with a liberal shaking of salt.

This highlights the value of diversifying your information sources. First, if the data are suspect, you're likely to read about it in the press. For example, it is widely understood that Argentine inflation figures are fudged by the government.[23] Second, third-party providers will often adjust their estimates for such inconsistencies.

Certainly, data credibility issues make it more difficult to objectively assess emerging markets. Unfortunately, there is no way to completely circumvent potential issues—it remains an inherent risk to investing in the category. But remaining diligent and inquisitive in your information gathering should help you stay ahead.

Chapter Recap

Properly identifying portfolio drivers is crucial to investing success. This is especially so in emerging markets, where countries and sectors perform vastly different from each other year to year and leadership changes often. To be successful, investors must identify information not widely known or interpret widely known information differently from other market participants and always frame forecasts in terms of supply and demand.

- Identifying portfolio drivers begins with an analysis of three broad categories of factors: economics, politics, and sentiment.
- These factors work across all categories of stocks, but the drivers within them will vary considerably depending on both place and time. (See the questions provided in this chapter to get a better understanding of what to look for in emerging markets.)
- This framework can also be applied to emerging markets as a category, although several key factors play particularly important roles at this level (like economic growth and the overall risk environment).
- Obtaining the required information to develop drivers is easier than ever. Investors can access a variety of websites—from government data sources to third-party newswires—with a simple Internet connection.
- Data quality issues remain, but diligent investors can navigate with little trouble.

7

SECURITY ANALYSIS

Turn on the television during market hours and there's a good chance you'll stumble across a purported expert expounding the virtues of some company's stock. Any number of reasons may be presented, but their focus will invariably be stock-specific—talk of supply and demand of securities or the importance of country and sector allocations is unlikely. That's because most investors believe investing begins and ends with picking stocks. Unfortunately, they're only half right.

As a top-down investor, you know the last step is indeed stock selection. But you also know it's the *least* important decision for your portfolio's overall return, and your investment process shouldn't start with it. This is especially so for emerging markets. As discussed in Chapter 5, emerging markets are concentrated. A few countries dominate the market, and a few sectors and stocks rule the country. This makes the top-down method the most logical approach because the largest companies—which often compose the majority of the country's weight—are often driven more by the economic, political, and sentiment drivers of the country than those specific to the company.

With the majority of excess return added in these higher level decisions, it's not vital to pick the "best" stocks in the universe. Rather, you want to pick stocks with a good probability of outperforming their peers. Doing so can enhance returns without jeopardizing good top-down decisions by picking risky, go-big-or-go-home stocks. Being right more often than not should create outperformance relative to your benchmark over time.

Every firm and every stock is different, and viewing them through the right lens is vital. Much like for portfolio drivers, investors need a functional, consistent, and reusable framework for analyzing securities. While by no means comprehensive, the framework provided and the questions at this chapter's end should serve as good starting points for the beginner-to-intermediate investor to help identify strategic attributes and company-specific risks. For a more thorough understanding of financial statement analysis, valuations, modeling, and other tools of security analysis, additional reading is suggested.

MAKE YOUR SELECTION

Security analysis is nowhere near as complicated as it may seem—but that doesn't mean it's easy. Similar to your goal in appropriately allocating to countries and sectors, you've got one basic task: Spot opportunities not currently discounted into prices. Or, put differently, know something others don't. Investors should analyze firms by taking consensus expectations for a company's estimated financial results and then assessing whether it will perform below, in line with, or above those baseline expectations. Profit opportunities arise when your expectations are different and more accurate than consensus expectations. Trading on widely known information or consensus expectations adds no value to the stock selection process. Doing so is really no different than trading on a coin flip.

The top-down method offers two ways to spot such opportunities. First, accurately predict high-level, macro themes affecting a group of companies—these are your portfolio drivers as outlined in Chapter 6. Second, find firms that will benefit most if those high-level themes and drivers play out. This is done by finding firms with competitive advantages (we'll explain this concept more in a bit).

A FIVE-STEP PROCESS

Analyzing a stock against its peer group can be summarized as a five-step process:

1. Understand business and earnings drivers.
2. Identify strategic attributes.
3. Analyze fundamental and stock price performance.
4. Identify risks.
5. Analyze valuations and consensus expectations.

These five steps provide a consistent framework for analyzing firms in their peer groups. While these steps are far from a full stock analysis, they provide the basics necessary to begin making better stock selections.

Step 1: Understand Business and Earnings Drivers

The first step is to understand what the business does, how it generates its earnings, and what drives those earnings. Here are a few tips to help in the process.

- **Industry overview**: Begin any analysis with a basic understanding of the firm's industry, including its drivers and risks. You should be familiar with how current economic trends affect the industry.
- **Company description**: Obtain a business description of the company, including an understanding of the products and services within each business segment. Browse the firm's website and financial statements/reports to gain an overview of the company and how it presents itself.
- **Corporate history**: An understanding of firm history may reveal its growth strategy or clues to its true core competencies. Analyze the firm's history since its inception and over the last several years. Ask questions like: Has it been an industry leader for decades, or is it a relative newcomer? Has it switched strategies or businesses often in the past?

- **Business segments**: Break down company revenues and earnings by business segment and geography to determine how and where it makes its money. Find out what drives results in each business and geographic segment. Begin thinking about how each of these business segments fits into your high-level themes.
- **Recent news/press releases**: Read all recently released news about the stock, including press releases. Do an Internet search and see what comes up. Look for any significant announcements regarding company operations. What is the media's opinion of the firm? Is it a bellwether to the industry or a minor player?
- **Markets and customers**: Identify main customers and the markets it operates in. Determine whether the firm has any particularly large single customer or a concentrated customer base.
- **Competition**: Find the main competitors and how market share compares with other industry players. Is the industry highly segmented? Assess the industry's competitive landscape. Keep in mind the biggest competitors can sometimes lurk in different industries—sometimes even in different sectors! Get a feel for how the firm stacks up—is it an industry leader or a minor player? Does market share matter in that industry?

Step 2: Identify Strategic Attributes

After gaining a sound grasp of firm operations, the next step is identifying strategic attributes consistent with higher level portfolio themes. Also known as competitive or comparative advantages, strategic attributes are unique features allowing firms to outperform their industry or sector. Since industry peers are generally affected by the same high-level drivers, strong strategic attributes are the edge in creating superior performance. Examples of strategic attributes include:

- High relative market share
- Low-cost production
- Superior sales relationships/distribution
- Economic sensitivity

- Vertical integration
- Strong management/business strategy
- Geographic diversity or advantage
- Consolidator
- Strong balance sheet
- Niche market exposure
- Pure play
- Potential takeover target
- Proprietary technologies
- Strong brand name
- First mover advantage

Strategic Attributes: Making Lemonade

How do strategic attributes help you analyze individual stocks? Consider a simple example: There are five lemonade stands of similar size, product, and quality within a city block. A scorching heat wave envelops the city, sending a rush of customers in search of lemonade. Which stand benefits most from the industry-wide surge in business? This likely depends on each stand's strategic attributes. Maybe one is a cost leader and has cheapest access to homegrown lemons. Maybe one has a geographic advantage and is located next to a basketball court full of thirsty players. Or maybe one has a superior business strategy with a "buy two, get one free" initiative that drives higher sales volume and a bigger customer base. Any of these are core strategic advantages.

Portfolio drivers help determine which kind of strategic attributes are likely to face head- or tailwinds. After all, not all strategic attributes will benefit a firm in all environments. For example, while higher operating leverage might help a firm boost earnings when an industry is booming, it would have the opposite effect in a down cycle. Access to iron ore reserves for a steel producer was an important strategic attribute from 2003 to 2007 due to the rising cost of raw materials (see Chapter 6). When iron ore prices decline, however, iron ore operations will create a drag on company earnings growth relative to other producers. Thus, it's essential to pick strategic attributes consistent with higher level portfolio themes.

A strategic attribute is also only effective to the extent management recognizes and takes advantage of it. Execution is key. For example, if a firm's strategic attribute is technological expertise, it should focus its effort on research and development to maintain that edge. If its strategic attribute is low-cost production relative to its peer group, it should capitalize by potentially lowering prices or expanding production (assuming the new production is also low cost) to gain market share.

Identifying strategic attributes may require thorough research of the firm's financial statements, website, news stories, history, and discussions with customers, suppliers, competitors, or management. Don't skimp on this step—be diligent and thorough in finding strategic attributes. It may feel like an arduous task at times, but it's also among the most important in security selection.

Step 3: Analyze Fundamental and Stock Price Performance

Once you've gained a thorough understanding of the business, earnings drivers, and strategic attributes, the next step is analyzing firm performance both fundamentally and in the stock market.

Emerging market financial information can be notoriously difficult to find. Reporting standards are simply not as rigorous and standardized as the developed world—countries often don't require regular filings, if at all. All is not lost, however. Most reasonably sized emerging market firms have listings on developed market exchanges. If a company lists on a US exchange, for example, it is required to file a 20-F—a condensed version of the 10-K filing, which is required annually for all US companies. These filings and more can be found online at the Securities and Exchange Commission's (SEC) EDGAR database (http://www.sec.gov/). In addition, as companies expand globally, they are increasingly cognizant of investors' desire to have detailed information on their financial results. As such, many companies have begun to post this information to their websites.

If you can't find information, ignore the company. Every once in a while, you may lose out on a winner, but it's simply not worth the added risk. If filings are available, analyze performance in recent quarters/years. Not all earnings results are created equal. Understanding what drives results gives clues to what will drive future performance. Ask things like:

- What are recent revenue trends? Earnings? Margins? Which business segments are seeing rising or falling sales?
- Is the firm growing its business organically, because of acquisitions, or some other reason?
- How sustainable is their strategy?
- Are earnings growing because of strong demand or because of cost cutting?
- Are they using tax loopholes and one-time items?
- What is management's strategy to grow the business for the future?
- What is the financial health of the company?

Next, evaluate stock performance. Check the company's chart for the last few years and try to determine what has driven performance. Explain any big up or down moves and identify any significant news events. If the stock price has trended steadily downward despite consistently beating earnings estimates, there may be a force driving the whole industry downward. Likewise, if the company's stock soared despite reporting tepid earnings growth or prospects, there may be some force driving the industry higher, like takeover speculation. Or stocks can simply move in sympathy with the broader market. Whatever it is, make sure you know and understand.

Some companies offer earnings calls announcing recent results. If available, these are typically posted on the investor relations section of a firm's website. They are invaluable—read as many as you can get your hands on. You'll begin to notice similar trends and events affecting the industry. Take note of these so you can distinguish between issues that are company-specific or industry-wide.

Step 4: Identify Risks

Emerging markets individually can be riskier than developed markets. This is well known. But the risks aren't terribly different from those in developed markets—it's the degree that varies. For example, there is a greater propensity for stock ownership to be concentrated in emerging markets. One individual, or even the government, owning a majority of shares is common.

There are two main types of risks in security analysis: stock-specific risk and systematic risk (also known as non–stock specific risk). Both can be equally important to performance.

Stock-specific risks, as the name suggests, are issues affecting the company in isolation. These are mainly risks affecting a firm's business operations or future operations. Some company-specific risks are discussed in detail in the annual reports, or regulatory filings, but one can't rely solely on firms self-identifying risk factors. You must see what analysts are saying about them and identify all risks for yourself. Other examples include:

- Stock ownership concentration (insider or institutional)
- Customer concentration
- Sole suppliers
- Excessive leverage or lack of access to financing
- Obsolete products
- Poor operational track record
- High cost of products versus competitors
- Latest filings
- Qualified audit opinions
- Hedging activities
- Pension or benefit underfunding risk
- Regulatory or legal (pending litigation)
- Pending corporate actions
- Executive departures
- Regional, political/governmental risk

Systematic risks include macroeconomic or geopolitical events out of a company's control—many of the potential drivers discussed in

Chapter 6. While these risks may affect a broad set of firms, they will have varying effects on each. Some examples include:

- Commodity prices
- Industry cost inflation
- Economic activity
- Labor scarcity
- Strained supply chain
- Legislation affecting taxes, royalties, or subsidies
- Geopolitical risks
- Capital expenditures
- Interest rates
- Currency
- Weather

Identifying stock-specific risks helps an investor evaluate the relative risk and reward potential of firms within a peer group. Identifying systematic risks helps you make informed decisions about which sub-industries and countries to overweight or underweight.

If you don't feel strongly about any company in a peer group within a sub-industry you wish to overweight, you could pick the company with the least stock-specific risk. This would help to achieve the goal of picking firms with the greatest probability of outperforming their peer group and still performing in line with your higher level themes and drivers.

Step 5: Analyze Valuations and Consensus Expectations

Valuations can be tricky. They are tools used to evaluate market sentiment and expectations for firms. But they are not a foolproof way to see if a stock is "cheap" or "expensive." Valuations are primarily used to compare firms against their peer group (or peer average) or a company's valuation relative to its own history. As mentioned earlier, stocks move not on the expected, but on the unexpected. We aim to try and gauge what the consensus expects for a company's future performance and then assess whether that company will perform below, in line with, or above expectations.

Valuations provide little information by themselves in predicting future stock performance. Just because one company's P/E is 20 while another's is 10 doesn't mean you should buy the one at 10 because it's "cheaper." There's likely a reason why one company has a different valuation than another, including such things as strategic attributes, earnings expectations, sentiment, stock-specific risks, and management's reputation. The main usefulness of valuations is explaining why a company's valuation differs from its peers and determining if it's justified.

There are many different valuation metrics investors use in security analysis. Some of the most popular include:

- P/E—price-to-earnings
- P/FE—price-to-forward earnings
- P/B—price-to-book
- P/S—price-to-sales
- P/CF—price-to-cash-flow
- DY—dividend yield
- EV/EBITDA—enterprise value to earnings before interest, taxes, depreciation, and amortization

Once you've compiled the valuations for a peer group, try to estimate why there are relative differences and if they're justified. Is a company's relatively low valuation due to stock-specific risk or low confidence from investors? Is the company's forward P/E relatively high because consensus is wildly optimistic about the stock? A firm's higher valuation may be entirely justified, for example, if it has a growth rate greater than its peers. A lower valuation may be warranted for a company facing a challenging operating environment in which it is losing market share. Seeing valuations in this way will help to differentiate firms and spot potential opportunities or risks.

Valuations should be used in combination with previous analysis of a company's fundamentals, strategic attributes, and risks. For example, Figure 7.1 is a grid showing how an investor could combine an analysis of strategic attributions and valuations to help pick firms.

	Valuation Low	Valuation High
Relatively Attractive	Best	
Relatively Unattractive		Worst

Strategic Attributes

Figure 7.1   Strategic Attributions & Valuation

Stocks with relatively low valuations but attractive strategic attributes may be underappreciated by the market (as shown in Figure 7.1). Stocks with relatively high valuations but no discernible strategic attributes may be overvalued by the market. Either way, use valuations appropriately and in the context of a larger investment opinion about a stock, not as a panacea for true value.

OTHER IMPORTANT QUESTIONS TO ASK

While this chapter's framework can be used to analyze any firm, there are additional factors related to emerging markets stocks that should be considered. The following section provides some of the most important factors and questions to consider when researching firms in the category. Answers to these questions should help distinguish between firms within a peer group and help identify strategic attributes and stock-specific risks. While there are countless other questions and factors that could and should be asked, these should serve as a good starting point.

> **Revenues and Earnings Breakdown**: Most firms produce more than a single product. The more diversified the revenue, the less exposed the firm is to fluctuations in a single product or end market. Its product mix will also determine what has the greatest affect on the firm's future earnings and performance. How are the firm's revenues and earnings divided between products? How does this compare to competitors? Is it more concentrated or diversified?

> **Geographic Breakdown and Geopolitical Risk**: Regional prices and volumes demanded can vary dramatically between home

and export markets. Thus, regional diversification can mitigate risks of big changes in any one market. For globally priced goods, a breakdown of regional production will help identify political and social risks to production, while a breakdown of regional consumption will identify the primary drivers.

Where are most of the firm's current and future planned production sites? Are they in politically stable or unstable countries? What percentage of production comes from politically unstable regions? Do they have a solid history of operating in foreign territories? Has the company historically had good or troubled relations with governments in the region? Are labor unions historically strong or weak in those regions? Do tariffs, subsidies, or price caps exist? Is the firm beholden to trade problems with other regions? For regionally priced goods, how quickly is the product's end market growing in its regions of operation?

While a firm with relatively high exposure to a geopolitically unstable region may face higher risks of government intervention or production disruption, the potential additions to production growth may warrant these risks and are not always inherent negatives.

Government Control: Emerging market governments play a larger role in firms. Companies are often partially or entirely government-owned and may be subject to unique taxes, royalties, subsidies, or price controls. Dividend policies may also be set in the interest of balancing budgets rather than future earnings. Depending on the circumstances, government ownership can work for or against a company, but you'll want to know its impact.

Some questions to ask: Are the firm's shares owned or controlled by a government? If so, to what degree? Does the government play an active role in firm decisions and policies? If so, has it ever made decisions in conflict with the interests of shareholders? Does the firm secure free market pricing for its product or does the government set pricing? Has the company historically been given special treatment or favored over other producers for contracts, loans, or taxes?

Competition and Barriers to Entry: What is the competitive landscape of the firm's peers? Does it compete against government-owned firms? Does the firm operate in a region or industry with significant barriers to entry? Barriers to entry may include dominant market share, capital intensity, patents, proprietary technology, a concentrated industry, and difficulty in obtaining regulatory or environmental permits. High barriers to entry typically provide pricing power and reduce competition.

Supply/Demand Environment: For globally priced goods, what is the product's supply/demand environment around the world? And for regionally priced goods, what is it within the firm's countries of operation? Have prices recently been affected by changes or expectations of changes in the supply/demand equation? Both supply- and demand-side factors will have a great influence on prices, which can be volatile.

Cost Structure: Emerging market firms tend to have notably different cost structures. Because firms often lack productivity-enhancing technology, labor costs are higher as a percent of revenue. These factors differ markedly across countries and sectors. What factors are driving the firm's production costs? What are the firm's production costs relative to its peers? What is the firm's strategy to mitigate industry cost inflation? Does its plan differ from competitors? If it's a low-cost producer compared to peers, does it have a strategy to take advantage of that? If it's a high-cost producer, does it have a strategy to change that?

Infrastructure: Emerging markets infrastructure varies across countries and is generally inferior to developed markets. Does the firm face infrastructure burdens relative to its peers? For example, does it have consistent access to electricity and power? Does it have easy access to its supply chain?

Transportation: Transportation costs are particularly important for bulk goods (with lower value-to-weight ratios) where transportation makes up a greater percentage of overall costs. How does the firm deliver its product to consumers? How far away are its consumers? What impact will rising or falling transportation costs have on it compared to competitors? Are there any transportation bottlenecks? If so, does it have a plan to address them? How has the firm responded to such bottlenecks in the past?

Legislative Risks: Are there any legislative risks? These can include royalties, windfall taxes, environmental legislation, price caps, labor laws, subsidies, tariffs, and the nationalization of assets. How thoroughly are laws enforced?

Technology and Innovation: Does the firm possess any proprietary technologies or patents giving it a competitive edge? Does it have a history of innovation? Is its end market dynamic, requiring the consistent release of new products, or do they specialize in more mature markets?

Regulation: How are the firm's operations affected by regulation? Does the firm currently operate in a favorable regulatory environment? How might that change? What is the firm's history with gaining regulatory approval for its products? Firms with highly regulated assets are exposed to regulatory risks, but they may also have more stable returns.

Market Share: Dominant market share often provides greater pricing power, especially for regionally priced goods. Because there are fewer companies competing in emerging market industries, dominant share levels differ from developed markets. For example, a company with a 20 percent share would likely have dominant share in the developed world but be an average-sized player in emerging markets.

Some questions to ask: What is the firm's market share in each of its business segments relative to its competitors? How fragmented are the consumers in its end markets? Does the firm have pricing power for its products and services? For regionally priced products, how do its prices and raw material costs compare to competitors?

Margins: Are margins growing or shrinking? Has the company historically offset higher costs with higher prices? How do its margins compare to peers? High margins in a vacuum tell you little since some industries historically hold higher margins than others, and it's usually well-known and taken into account in share prices.

Cash-Flow Use: How is the firm spending its cash flow? To what degree is it buying back shares, paying dividends, spending on capital expenditures, or paying down debt? Depending on industry conditions, investors may prefer a firm rewarding shareholders with dividends and share buybacks over one taking on risky new production plans.

Balance Sheet: Does the firm have the financial ability to make large acquisitions to fuel growth? Does the firm's balance sheet allow it to take on additional leverage? Debt isn't necessarily a bad thing—many firms generate an excellent return on borrowed funds. In either case, it's vital to understand the capital structure of a firm.

Interest Rates: Interest rates vary widely across countries and industries. How sensitive is the firm's operations to interest rates? Are rising or falling rates good or bad for the firm's operations and share price? Firms with greater leverage tend to be more affected by interest rate movements due to changes in interest expense.

Currency: Currency risk arises when a company sells it goods or services to a foreign country. How much of the company's revenues are denominated in foreign currency? What are the risks in that foreign country? Is the company hedged?

Employee Relations: What is the company's relationship with its workforce? Is it heavily unionized? Generous pension benefits? Lifetime employment? Can a company freely hire or fire workers based on the country's employment laws? Labor laws can have a dramatic impact on the operating environment (like Black Economic Empowerment (BEE) in Chapter 4).

Security Availability: Last, but certainly not least, can you actually purchase the security through your broker? Is an ADR available?

Chapter Recap

In the top-down investment process, stocks are largely tools to leverage higher-level themes, or portfolio drivers. Once an attractive segment of the market is identified, investors should attempt to determine the firms most likely to outperform their peers by finding those with strategic attributes. The five-step security selection process detailed in this chapter provides a guide, and the questions at its end get you started. But don't limit yourself to just these—the more questions you ask, the better your analysis will be.

- The top-down investment methodology first identifies and analyzes high-level portfolio drivers affecting broad categories of stocks. These drivers help determine portfolio country, sector, and style weights.
- Quantitative factor screening helps narrow the list of potential portfolio holdings based on characteristics such as valuations, liquidity, and solvency.
- Stock selection is the last step in the top-down process. Stock selection attempts to find companies possessing strategic attributes consistent with higher level portfolio drivers.
- Stock selection also attempts to find companies with the greatest probability of outperforming their peers.

PUTTING IT TOGETHER

The preceding chapters provided knowledge necessary to confidently invest in emerging markets. But all that preparation means little if you don't know how to put it to use. Our last chapter focuses on practical concerns for investing in emerging markets, including the instruments available, different strategies, and the unique challenges in this corner of the investing universe. We then depart with a brief nod to the next frontier of emerging markets.

TWO INITIAL CONSIDERATIONS

Before detailing the tools, however, there are two important preliminary considerations: the type of investor you are and the strategy you intend to employ.

Institutional versus Retail

There are essentially two broad categories of investors—*retail* and *institutional.* Institutional investors are the big fish of the investment world. They wield hundreds of millions or billions of dollars and generally have a dedicated research staff and even trading desk to implement their portfolios. Their clients are huge foundations, endowments, and pension plans.

Retail investors, on the other hand, are the minnows of the investing universe. They have portfolios in the thousands of dollars up to a few million. They generally access their accounts online, place trades electronically or over the phone with a broker, and generally conduct their own research. Or they may hire a professional—usually one who specializes in working with other retail investors.

Most people are retail investors. But don't let that make you feel inferior—minnows can still swim. Twenty years ago, investing in emerging markets was a cumbersome affair. Access to local markets was difficult and only institutions with custodial and trading contacts across the globe could efficiently invest. A lack of data other than broad index information also hindered proper due diligence and reporting. Retail investors were at an even greater disadvantage. For them, hiring a professional money manager was virtually the only option for emerging markets exposure.

Many of these barriers have crumbled. Professional money managers still provide worthwhile services for those without the time or confidence to do it themselves, but a range of new instruments, like American Depositary Receipts (ADRs) and exchange-traded funds (ETFs), offer alternatives. Today, retail investors can easily construct a wide variety of strategies on their own. The chasm between the capabilities of an institutional and retail investor has narrowed considerably.

Passive versus Active

For either type of investor, there are two broad investment strategies—*passive* or *active*. At the broadest level, an active approach tries to outperform a benchmark by intentionally deviating from it. If you have a particularly positive outlook for a specific country or sector, for example, you may *overweight* it relative to the benchmark, and vice versa. Conversely, you can *underweight* areas you have less positive outlooks for. (Recall Chapter 6 for a refresher.)

A passive approach, on the other hand, tries to make a portfolio mirror the respective benchmark as much as possible. For instance, a passive emerging markets investor would allocate 8.4 percent to South

African stocks, 5.2 percent to Mexico, and 18.2 percent to China (see Table 5.1 for these weights). He'd also invest 22.8 percent of his portfolio to Financials stocks and 7.7 percent to Industrials (see Table 5.2). A passive approach thus *neutral weights* all categories of stocks relative to the benchmark.

The instruments used will depend on your approach. A passive approach frequently means eschewing individual stocks for instruments with broader market exposure like mutual funds or ETFs. (An ETF is a passive investment that mimics the performance of a specific benchmark; more on this in a bit.) But this doesn't necessarily mean a passive approach requires no work—investors must carefully monitor exposure and rebalance periodically.

An active approach utilizes a broader range of instruments. Individual stocks usually play a predominate role. But investors may also use *passive investments* to create an active strategy. How so? Imagine an investor builds an all-ETF portfolio. Is it a passive strategy if a portfolio is made up entirely of passive investments? Not necessarily. In our example, rather than own ETFs precisely to the weight in the benchmark, such as 5.2 percent allocation to Mexico's ETF (EWW), an investor could hold more or less depending on his view of the country. If you were particularly bullish on Mexico, you could allocate 10 percent of your portfolio to EWW, a notable overweight to the benchmark. This is an *active allocation* (country bet) using a *passive investment*.

Many tools used today are common across all categories. But each case—institutional versus retail and passive versus active—calls for slightly different considerations. Next, we more closely evaluate the instruments at emerging markets investors' disposal.

INSTRUMENTS FOR INVESTING IN EMERGING MARKETS

There are essentially four major types of investments for most emerging markets investors: mutual funds, exchange-traded funds, depositary receipts, and ordinary shares. We begin with those instruments most applicable to any type of investor.

Depositary Receipts and Ordinary Shares

We discussed the basics of security selection in Chapter 7. If you've decided to dive full bore into emerging markets and pick your own stocks, there are two distinct types of shares at your disposal—*ordinary shares* or *depositary receipts*.

Ordinary Shares   *Ordinary shares* are exactly what they sound like—plain-vanilla, individual stocks. If you're an American, living in America, and you pick up the phone to place an order for a US stock, you're buying an ordinary share. Investors can also buy foreign ordinaries—foreign stocks traded on a country's local exchange—although matters can be complicated by other considerations, such as trading laws, regulations, and where and how you custody them.

Once an option only to institutions, foreign ordinaries are becoming increasingly available to the average investor. Most full-service brokers can access ordinary shares in foreign markets for clients. And discount brokerages have started to offer the securities. Clients of Charles Schwab & Co. can access stocks in 45 foreign countries, and E*Trade Securities now offers online trading in six foreign markets and five currencies.

The drawbacks to buying foreign ordinaries? They can be costly. There are usually several layers of fees: the commission charged by your broker, fees to convert currency, foreign broker fees, and taxes and other charges levied directly by foreign governments. These fees can be an onerous hurdle for retail and even smaller institutional investors—the cost of buying stocks in some countries can exceed 10 percent of your investment. Thus, be sure to fully evaluate transaction costs before purchasing these types of stocks.

Depositary Receipts   Depositary receipts (DRs) offer an alternative. Depository banks, such as JP Morgan, Bank of New York, and Deutsche Bank, collect ordinary shares and issue DRs into the local market. As such, they represent shares issued by a foreign company but on a local exchange. Each DR is backed by a set number of ordinary shares trading in the firm's home market, but the number of shares represented isn't necessarily one-to-one. For example, owning a single *American Depositary Receipt* (ADR) in the Taiwanese semiconductor company Taiwan Semiconductor Manufacturing (TSM) is equivalent to owning five ordinary shares.

Depositary receipts come in all forms depending on the listed exchange. For example, *Global Depositary Receipts* (aka GDRs) trade on exchanges in London, Luxembourg, Frankfurt, Dubai, and Singapore, among others. But the most common are ADRs—shares of foreign companies listed on a US exchange.

For most retail investors, owning ADRs can be the easiest and most cost-effective way to gain exposure to foreign stocks. ADRs are scarcely different than owning US stocks—many are registered with the Securities and Exchange Commission (SEC), pay ADR holders dividends in US dollars, and follow US accounting and reporting standards. Custody issues are also fewer because shares are held at large, reputable US institutions.

ADRs aren't just for retail investors, either. If a company has both an ADR and an ordinary share, there's a good chance the ADR will be cheaper. Buying ordinary shares may be easy, but transaction costs are generally higher outside of the US. Since ADRs are listed on US exchanges, all investors can take advantage of the lower costs here.

There are four types of ADRs, each with different listing requirements:

- **Level I**: The most basic ADRs. Level I ADRs aren't listed on US exchanges, but instead trade *over-the-counter*. As a result, most have five-letter tickers ending in "Y." Because Level I ADRs are the easiest and least costly for a company to list, they're also the most abundant. But that means investors need to pay close attention to liquidity—many aren't actively traded.
- **Level II**: Companies listing Level II ADRs file a registration statement with the SEC. They must file annual reports and follow US accounting standards. Level II ADRs are also listed on exchanges, conferring greater visibility and trading volume.

- **Level III**: Level III ADRs require the most work for foreign firms. Issuing Level I and II ADRs means taking shares from the local market, giving them to a depository institution, and releasing ADR shares. By contrast, Level III ADRs represent entirely new shares to be put on deposit. Therefore, they require many of the same regulatory steps as a new share offering by a US firm.
- **144A**: Available only to Qualified Institutional Buyers. This is a market for professional investors only, making reporting requirements relatively lax.

Unfortunately, not every foreign company has a depositary receipt. In fact, some of the largest companies in emerging markets (and the world) don't have them, so the only way to own these securities is through ordinary shares. JP Morgan offers a comprehensive search tool of all available DRs at www.adr.com.

Exchange-Traded Funds (ETFs)

Exchange-traded funds also represent an important tool to both retail and institutional investors. ETFs share many of the same attributes as index funds—namely lower costs and efficient diversification (more on index funds in a bit). But there is one major difference. While mutual funds are priced only once a day (at the market's close), ETFs trade intraday like a stock. This subjects them to different standards. ETFs must report holdings daily, giving them greater transparency.

ETFs allow investors to make fairly precise investment decisions while reducing stock-specific risk. This can be especially useful for emerging markets. For example, Thailand accounts for 1.4 percent of the MSCI Emerging Markets Index (see Table 5.1). Since it's a relatively small portion of the index, a bullish investor might only buy a stock or two to overweight the country. But that leaves the investor exposed to stock-specific risk. Instead, he could buy the iShares MSCI Thailand (THD), an ETF tracking the broad Thai market, and effectively eliminate this risk.

Table 8.1   Select ETFs With Emerging Market Exposure

Broad	Regional	Country
SPDR MSCI ACWI ex-US (CWI)	SPDR S&P Emerging Asia Pacific (GMF)	SPDR S&P China (GXC)
SPDR S&P Emerging Markets (GMM)	SPDR S&P Emerging Latin America (GML)	iShares FTSE/Xinhua China 25 (FXI)
iShares MSCI ACWI (ACWI)	SPDR S&P Emerging Europe (GUR)	iShares FTSE China (HK Listed) (FCHI)
iShares MSCI ACWI ex-US (ACWX)	SPDR S&P BRIC 40 (BIX)	iShares MSCI Brazil (EWZ)
iShares MSCI Emerging Markets (EEM)	SPDR S&P Emerging Middle East & Africa (GAF)	iShares MSCI Chile (ECH)
	iShares S&P Latin America 40 (ILF)	iShares MSCI Israel (EIS)
	iShares MSCI BRIC (BKF)	iShares MSCI Malaysia (EWM)
	iShares MSCI All Country Asia ex Japan (AAXJ)	iShares MSCI Mexico (EWW)
	iShares S&P Asia 50 (AIA)	iShares MSCI South Africa (EZA)
		iShares MSCI South Korea (EWY)
		iShares MSCI Taiwan (EWT)
		iShares MSCI Thailand (THD)
		iShares MSCI Turkey (TUR)

Source: iShares; SPDRS.com.

There is a dizzying array of ETFs available to emerging market investors. Table 8.1 lists those from two well-known ETF providers—Barclays (iShares) and State Street Global Advisors (SPDRs). Other providers offer more, but no matter which one you choose, there are funds for all types of investors and strategies. For example, investors desiring simple, broad exposure can purchase a fund like the iShares MSCI All-Country World Index (ACWI), an index tracking performance of all developed and emerging markets. Others after more active management can utilize individual country and regional funds. For example, maybe you've done more analysis on Latin America and think you have a pretty good idea about how things work in that part of the world. But you don't know much about Eastern Europe or Asia and don't believe you have any particularly valuable insight into stocks there. You could purchase a fund for these regions (GMF and GUR) and then pick individual stocks for Latin America. Such permutations are endless.

Mutual Funds

Mutual funds are primarily a tool used by retail investors to gain access to a professional money manager. These services remain popular, and there are good reasons for this. Mutual funds are a one-stop shop—purchasing a fund gives an investor access to a team of analysts and trading and custodial contacts—taking the onus off the retail investor. They also benefit investors with smaller accounts because they offer diversification—an especially important consideration for volatile emerging markets—in one neatly packaged security.

But there are negatives. Mutual funds offer no customization. They're *commingled* assets, meaning investors' money is pooled together and managed as one large portfolio. Each investor gets the same stocks and allocation decisions as every other investor. This also means they are not tax efficient—investors don't get the benefit of realizing losses to offset gains at tax time. Mutual funds are also not particularly transparent. They are only required to report holdings once a quarter and often only divulge a detail or two about the manager.

Any big mutual fund company (e.g., Fidelity, Vanguard, Legg Mason) likely offers an emerging market fund. But before committing to one, investors should studiously evaluate candidates on several key points.

Fees   Mutual funds can be costly. And emerging market funds especially so. Expect to pay an *expense ratio* north of 1 to 1.25 percent a year or more for an actively managed emerging market fund—slightly more expensive than a developed market fund. Higher fees relative to other asset classes should be expected—it's more costly to gather emerging market data and transaction costs can be higher.

Not only can fees be higher, but they vary widely, too. For example, the US Global Investors Emerging Markets Fund (GEMFX) charges an expense ratio of 2.5 percent. By contrast, the T. Rowe Price Emerging Market Fund (PRMSX) charges nearly half that—1.27 percent.[1] Is the former twice the manager as the latter? Maybe, maybe not. The point is there can be wide variance, and you should evaluate the entire picture— an extra 1 percent a year is a lot of money. You want to be sure that's justified.

There's more. Many mutual funds may also have a *load*—a sales charge that's either tacked onto the initial purchase price ("front end"), deferred to when an investor sells the fund later on ("back end"), or charged annually ("level load"). The fund's share class determines the fee charged (e.g., A shares, B shares), and they vary depending on the provider. Some can be quite high, so evaluate each carefully. Other funds are "no load"—meaning they don't charge a sales commission. But that doesn't necessarily mean there are no expenses. No-load funds still have an expense ratio to cover operating costs. All of these fees, charges, commissions, and expenses are fully disclosed in each fund's prospectus, so be sure to review it and understand what you are paying and why—and whether you think it's worth it.

Allocation Decisions   Allocation decisions across mutual funds vary considerably. Actively managed mutual fund managers consciously deviate from their benchmarks. As an example, Tables 8.2 and 8.3 show country and sector weights of the T. Rowe Price fund (mentioned earlier) relative to the MSCI Emerging Markets Index, the fund's benchmark.

The differences in some areas can be vast. At the end of 2008, the manager appeared to be bullish on Latin America, with big over-weights to Mexico and Brazil relative to the benchmark. He also appeared relatively negative on Asia, with underweights to Malaysia, South Korea, and Taiwan. And he took a significant benchmark

Table 8.2   T. Rowe Price Emerging Market Fund Country Weights

Country	PRMSX Weight	MSCI EM Weight	Over/Underweight
Mexico	9.5%	5.2%	4.3%
Brazil	16.8%	12.9%	3.9%
Qatar	3.5%	0.0%	3.5%
Hong Kong	3.2%	0.0%	3.2%
Oman	2.0%	0.0%	2.0%
India	8.4%	6.5%	1.9%
Russia	7.0%	5.7%	1.3%
Egypt	1.6%	0.7%	0.9%
UK	0.9%	0.0%	0.9%
China	19.1%	18.2%	0.9%
Argentina	1.0%	0.1%	0.9%
Ukraine	0.2%	0.0%	0.2%
Bahrain	0.1%	0.0%	0.1%
Cyprus	0.0%	0.0%	0.0%
Peru	0.7%	0.7%	0.0%
Pakistan	0.0%	0.1%	−0.1%
Colombia	0.5%	0.6%	−0.1%
Philippines	0.0%	0.5%	−0.5%
Morocco	0.0%	0.5%	−0.5%
Hungary	0.0%	0.6%	−0.6%
Chile	0.6%	1.4%	−0.8%
Indonesia	0.7%	1.5%	−0.8%
Turkey	0.6%	1.5%	−0.9%
Czech Republic	0.0%	0.9%	−0.9%
Thailand	0.0%	1.4%	−1.4%
Israel	1.9%	3.4%	−1.5%
Poland	0.0%	1.6%	−1.6%
Malaysia	0.8%	3.0%	−2.3%
South Korea	10.6%	13.6%	−3.1%
Taiwan	7.3%	10.9%	−3.5%
South Africa	0.5%	8.4%	−7.9%

Source: Bloomberg Finance L.P., Thomson Datastream, MSCI, Inc.[2] as of 12/31/2008.

Table 8.3   T. Rowe Price Emerging Market Fund Sector Weights

Sector	PRMSX Weight	MSCI EM Weight	Over/Underweight
Consumer Staples	11.4%	5.8%	5.6%
Financials	28.2%	22.8%	5.4%
Consumer Disc.	8.2%	4.8%	3.5%
Industrials	10.8%	7.7%	3.1%
Health Care	0.9%	2.9%	−1.9%
Materials	10.3%	12.8%	−2.5%
Tech	8.1%	10.8%	−2.7%
Energy	11.3%	14.9%	−3.5%
Utilities	0.2%	4.0%	−3.8%
Telecom.	8.3%	13.6%	−5.3%

Source: Bloomberg Finance L.P., Thomson Datastream, MSCI, Inc.[3], as of 12/31/2008.

deviation to South Africa—owning only one company at 0.5 percent for nearly an 8 percent underweight.

Note too there quite a few holdings from countries outside the benchmark. For example, 3.5 percent of the fund is invested in Qatar, which is not considered an emerging market by MSCI (it's a *frontier market*—more on this later). The fund even has developed market stocks, with 3.2 percent allocated to Hong Kong and 0.9 percent to the UK. While these allocations may be small, deviating from the benchmark can subject investors to a different set of risks and drivers.

From a sector standpoint, the manager appeared to have several areas of high conviction. He took more than a 5 percent overweight to Consumer Staples and Financials—likely because he expects these areas to outperform. By contrast, he appears relatively down on Utilities and Telecom stocks, with underweights there.

Most active mutual fund managers will make similar decisions—deviating from their benchmark with over- and underweights to particular regions, countries, sectors, even sizes and styles. Just remember hiring a manager means ceding allocation decisions to someone else, which can lead to wide divergence from your benchmark you won't necessarily be able to control.

This concept becomes especially important if investors purchase more than one mutual fund in the same category. While it's likely one fund will look different from another, it's also possible it holds many of the same allocations. Unwittingly, an investor could double up on a particular country, sector, or stock, decreasing diversification advantages. Since allocations change over time with active management, it's important for investors to monitor these types of exposure.

Index Funds   Not all mutual funds are active. John Bogle, founder of the Vanguard Group, created the first passive mutual fund in 1975, called an *index fund*.[4] Index funds have exploded in popularity over the years, and for good reason—they represent an easy vehicle to get market exposure to a specific category of stocks. The average retail investor probably won't have the time, tools, or capital to purchase every single security in a benchmark and then constantly monitor and rebalance. And since index funds are passive, expense ratios can be substantially lower than active funds. For example, Vanguard's Emerging Market Stock Index Fund (VEIEX) charges investors 0.32 percent. If the passive approach is your thing, index funds can be an appropriate tool.

Leveraged Funds   Leveraged mutual funds use derivatives to achieve some multiple of performance of the underlying index. For example, the ProFunds Ultra Emerging Markets Fund (UUPIX) attempts to achieve 200 percent of the daily performance of the Bank of New York Emerging Markets 50 ADR Index.[5] Though leveraged vehicles can amplify gains, losses are also potentially greater.

In addition, the time it takes to recoup losses with leveraged vehicles is longer than non-leveraged investments. Why? Returns are asymmetrical—a 25 percent rise does not erase a 25 percent decline. Imagine you own $1,000 in both an emerging market index fund and a leveraged emerging markets fund. The index falls 25 percent this year. The index fund thus falls 25 percent to $750, while the leveraged fund drops 50 percent to $500. Now imagine that markets rally 33 percent the following year. The index fund has recouped its losses and is now worth $1,000 again. What about the leveraged fund? Despite posting an eye-catching 66 percent return, it remains below the original value, at $833. In other words, because you lose more during the down periods, it takes longer to make it back. This makes leveraged funds especially risky during volatile periods.

COMMON CHALLENGES AND RISKS

Investing in emerging markets may be easier than ever, but challenges remain. A host of issues can make investing more expensive, risky, or just downright frustrating. Remaining cognizant of these matters will lead to fewer headaches later.

Liquidity

Liquidity refers generally to both the cost and ease of transacting in a particular security. A liquid market implies ready and willing buyers and sellers at all times and a high probability that the next executed trade is at a price equal or close to the last one. Such factors vary tremendously across stocks—some exchange hands many millions times each day, while others only trade a few times over the course of several weeks.

In general, emerging market stocks tend to trade less, making liquidity considerations particularly important. Table 8.4 shows the average daily trading volume across several developed and emerging markets. Most emerging market countries trade substantially less than their developed market peers. China, the most actively traded emerging market, still only has a third of the volume traded in the US. At the other end of the spectrum, Peru only trades $29 million a day.

Why does liquidity matter? Imagine you're the manager of a $1 billion portfolio with 100 stocks. To simplify, let's say each position is the same weight—1 percent of the portfolio, or $10 million. That may seem like quite a bit of money in one stock, but for big, developed

Table 8.4 Representative Dollar Trading Volume by Country

Country	Dollar Volume Trade (US$ Millions)
US	33,416
Japan	23,431
UK	13,176
China	11,310
Canada	6,088
Korea	3,282
Taiwan	2,845
Brazil	2,611
India	2,509
Mexico	417
Thailand	386
Indonesia	258
Malaysia	255
Argentina	140
Chile	125
Philippines	58
Peru	29

Figures are the average daily trading volume in US dollars of representative stock market exchanges for the 12 months ending April 22, 2009.

Source: Bloomberg Finance, L.P.

market stocks, it's often a drop in the bucket. For example, as of this writing, shares of General Electric (GE), the US industrial giant, traded on average 116 million shares a day at roughly $21 a share.[6] That means well over $2 *billion* in GE shares exchanged hands each day. A $10 million trade would hardly make a dent in the stock's daily volume.

Now imagine you're trying to purchase $10 million in Bank Pekao, a sizeable Polish bank ($11 billion market capitalization). The stock traded 571,000 shares a day at an average of $56 per share, equating to a little over $30 million in dollar volume.[7] Here, a $10 million trade would account for a substantial amount of one day's total volume. Since purchasing one-third of a stocks' daily volume at once would likely move the market price (sellers would match the sudden increase in demand with an increase in price), investors could spread the purchase out over the course of several days. But that also means it would take several days to sell out of the security later—the lack of liquidity compromises flexibility and quick action.

Market Depth

Market depth refers to the size of a trade needed to move a security's market price a given amount. If a market is *deep*, a large order is needed to change the price. If a market is *shallow*, a smaller trade can impact the market price. Market depth is synonymous with liquidity (i.e. a deep market is a liquid market).

Liquidity also matters because it affects transaction costs. With financial instruments (stocks, ETFs, currencies, etc.), the price one investor pays is usually more than another investor collects. The different prices are known as the *bid* and the *ask*, and the *bid-ask spread* varies depending on the supply and demand of the security. If a stock has relatively few shares trading (i.e., it's less liquid) the buyer will command a premium as compensation, resulting in a higher bid-ask spread. In our example, this cost is likely negligible for GE but might cause an investor to think twice about Bank Pekao.

Liquidity concerns aren't just a concern for institutional investors wielding large sums of money. Smaller retail investors will also face difficulties buying ordinary shares in smaller markets. Trading volumes for ADRs can be problematic as well—many Level I ADRs barely trade at all. In either case, a liquidity analysis should be conducted by all investors prior to trading any security.

Market Accessibility

If you're an institutional investor, it's relatively straightforward to gain access to most developed market stock exchanges. Fill out a few forms, pay a nominal fee, establish custodial accounts, and you're up and trading—for the most part. Local trading access is usually prohibitively expensive for individual retail investors, but they can easily leverage their broker's institutional contacts.

Similar access to emerging market exchanges, however, can be particularly onerous. Hefty fees, long waiting periods, strange and inconvenient requirements, shallow depositary markets, and many other impediments can make even the sanest investor question whether it's worth it.

Take investing in India. There are essentially two ways to invest in Indian shares: Register as a Foreign Institutional Investor (FII) to trade on India's domestic stock exchanges or buy depositary receipts. There are notable difficulties and expenses associated with both options.

To register as an FII, investors must submit an application with the Securities and Exchange Board of India (SEBI). The investor must pay a $10,000 registration fee every three years, and any sub-accounts managed by the investor—a common structure for institutional investors—must also register with the SEBI and pay a $2,000 registration fee.[8]

On top of the steep fees, the government limits the amount of shares FIIs can purchase. Individually, no one FII can own more than 10 percent of a company's outstanding shares. Sub-accounts can hold no more than 5 percent. And as a group, FII investment is capped at 24 percent.[9] All these restrictions mean the Indian ordinary market is relatively shallow. Less than 100 Indian stocks, out of more than 3,000 listed, make up roughly 75 percent of shares traded.[10]

With such a cumbersome and challenging road to investing in Indian ordinary shares, one might think the ADR universe would provide a suitable alternative. Not quite. Only 25 companies list ADRs and only 14 of those, listed in Table 8.5, trade with any volume on a US exchange. There simply aren't many options available to US investors—market accessibility is low.

Other markets pose different challenges. To trade Argentine ordinary shares, an account must be open with the central bank for a full year beforehand. Opening a custody account in Turkey costs several thousand dollars. Many similar hurdles exist in other nations.

Table 8.5   Indian ADRs Traded on US Exchanges

ADR Ticker	Company Name	Avg 30-Day Volume (Shares)
IBN	ICICI Bank	3,809,916
INFY	Infosys Technologies	3,023,756
SAY	Satyam Computer	2,915,845
TTM	Tata Motors	1,485,599
SLT	Sterlite Industries	1,267,412
WIT	Wipro Ltd	654,662
HDB	HDFC Bank	578,286
RDY	Dr. Reddy's	216,754
TCL	Tata Communications	148,202
SIFY	Sify Technologies	115,444
MTE	Mahanagar Telephone	65,358
PTI	Patni Computer	47,489
WNS	WNS Holdings	41,483
REDF	Rediff.com India	36,606

Source: Bloomberg Financial, L.P. as of 4/22/09.

Fortunately, the trend is toward greater market accessibility as governments increasingly recognize the benefits of open capital markets. But investors must evaluate these types of costs in each market before determining if an investment in individual stocks is appropriate.

Unexpected Market Closure

Developed market stock exchanges are reliably open for business—rarely do they close without warning. The same is not always true for emerging markets, where greater degrees of political, social, and economic volatility means markets often shutter unexpectedly, sometimes for extended periods. In late 2008, for example, Russian officials closed the local exchange on four separate occasions due to worries that intense selling pressure on the ruble and stock market threatened stability.[11] Clearly, such unpredictable action increases the risks associated with investing in ordinary shares—another reason owning depositary receipts may be preferable since they're not traded on local exchanges.

Repatriation Difficulties

Repatriating investments in emerging markets can also be potentially problematic. Most investors don't think twice about buying stocks in Canada or France—strong property rights in developed markets reassure investors will be able to send home the proceeds from their assets when the time comes to sell. The same cannot be said for some emerging markets, where property rights are notably weaker. While not common, there have been several historical instances where countries restricted the free flow of foreign investor capital.

For example, in the wake of the Asian Financial Crisis, trading in Malaysian ringgit instruments was banned as the government tried to stabilize markets. Officials then instituted a 12-month holding period on the repatriation of securities by foreign investors. That is, investors were unable to retrieve their money out of the country for a full year.[12] The government loosened restrictions several months later, but investors were still subject to hefty levies, up to 30 percent, if they withdrew money earlier than the 12-month period.[13] Thailand's government instituted similar capital controls following its 2006 coup d'état.

THE FUTURE—FRONTIER MARKETS

To some, emerging markets aren't quite emerging enough. As the asset class becomes more broadly accepted, investors are already scouring the globe for new opportunities. Recently, a new corner of the world—*frontier markets*—has gained in prominence. Frontier markets are generally less sophisticated than emerging markets across the characteristics detailed in Chapter 1. MSCI launched its Frontier Markets Index in 2007, consisting of 22 countries, from Kuwait to Bulgaria.

Tables 8.6 and 8.7 illustrate the country and sector weights of the index. These markets are even more concentrated than emerging markets. The four largest countries and one sector—Financials—account for roughly two-thirds of the index. Frontier markets are also only a tiny fraction of the global investment universe. Some perspective: The combined market cap of the MSCI Frontier Market Index represents 8.1 percent of the MSCI Emerging Markets Index and a miniscule 1.5 percent of the MSCI World Index. The largest company, Industries

Table 8.6   MSCI Frontier Markets Index Country Weights

Country	Weight	Country	Weight
Kuwait	35.6%	Bahrain	2.4%
Nigeria	11.7%	Vietnam	1.7%
United Arab Emirates (UAE)	11.6%	Romania	1.3%
Qatar	9.5%	Tunisia	0.9%
Kazakhstan	4.0%	Mauritius	0.9%
Jordan	3.8%	Estonia	0.4%
Oman	3.7%	Sri Lanka	0.3%
Slovenia	3.2%	Ukraine	0.2%
Kenya	2.9%	Serbia	0.2%
Croatia	2.7%	Lithuania	0.2%
Lebanon	2.7%	Bulgaria	0.1%

Source: Thomson Datastream, MSCI Inc.[14] as of 12/31/2008.

Table 8.7   MSCI Frontier Markets Index Sector Weights

Sector	Weight
Financials	61.7%
Telecommunication Services	12.8%
Industrials	7.0%
Energy	5.4%
Consumer Staples	4.4%
Materials	4.2%
Health Care	1.7%
Consumer Discretionary	1.2%
Utilities	1.1%
Information Technology	0.4%

Source: Thomson Datastream, MSCI Inc.[15] as of 12/31/2008.

Qatar, would rank as the 305th largest in the MSCI World Index and the 37th largest in the MSCI Emerging Markets. And Exxon Mobil's market capitalization is nearly one and a half times as large as the *entire* MSCI Frontier Market Index.[16]

In many ways, frontier markets are what emerging markets were like 20 years ago: data are limited, liquidity problematic, and overall support for foreign ownership and involvement in local stock exchanges low. In addition, capital flows are largely restricted and property rights tenuous at best. Much structural reform is needed for these countries to follow a similar path of development as emerging markets. Given weak political and regulatory institutions, such change is far from certain. Emerging markets will continue to develop, and some may move up to developed market status in the future. Just the same, some frontier markets may climb the ladder to emerging status. But for now, they represent some of the riskiest equity investments available—so consider whether it's appropriate for you when making portfolio decisions.

Wherever the investment future takes you, this book can serve as your guide. Learning to think about markets with the framework provided—from emerging markets to the next frontier—should increase your chances of success. Happy investing.

Chapter Recap

This last chapter focuses on putting previously accumulated knowledge to practical use.

- There are two primary types of investors—retail and institutional.
- Many instruments are available to both retail and institutional investors, from depositary receipts to exchange-traded funds.
  - How you use them depends on whether you take a passive or active approach.
- Investing in emerging markets is not without challenges—liquidity, structural issues, and overall low levels of property rights can make investing difficult for even the most seasoned investor.
- Emerging markets will continue to develop, and investors will seek out new frontiers. But the tools and methodologies discussed in this book can serve as a useful guide no matter how the investing world develops.

Notes

CHAPTER 1: THE FIVE Ws OF EMERGING MARKETS

1. Central Intelligence Agency, "The World Factbook," (July 15, 2009), https:// www.cia.gov/library/publications/the-world-factbook/index.html (accessed July 15, 2009).
2. Deborah Potter, "Handbook of Independent Journalism," (July 2006), http://www .america.gov/media/pdf/books/journalism.pdf#popup (accessed April 21, 2009).
3. Central Intelligence Agency, "The World Factbook," (July 15, 2009), https:// www.cia.gov/library/publications/the-world-factbook/index.html (accessed July 15, 2009); International Monetary Fund, "World Economic Outlook," (April 2009).   http://www.imf.org/external/pubs/ft/weo/2008/01/weodata/index.aspx (accessed April 21, 2009). Data are based on the "Emerging and developing economies" category as defined by the IMF.
4. Source: MSCI. The MSCI information may only be used for your internal use, may not be reproduced or redisseminated in any form and may not be used to create any financial instruments or products or any indices. The MSCI information is provided on an "as is" basis, and the user of this information assumes the entire risk of any use made of this information. MSCI, each of its affiliates and each other person involved in or related to compiling, computing, or creating any MSCI information (collectively, the "MSCI Parties") expressly disclaims all warranties (including, without limitation, any warranties of originality, accuracy, completeness, timeliness, non-infringement, merchant-ability, and fitness for a particular purpose) with respect to this information. Without limiting any of the foregoing, in no event shall any MSCI Party have any liability for any direct, indirect, special, incidental, punitive, consequential (including, without limitation, lost profits), or any other damages.
5. The World Bank, "Key Development Data & Statistics," http://web .worldbank.org/WBSITE/EXTERNAL/DATASTATISTICS/0,,contentMDK: 20535285~menu PK:1390200 ~pagePK:64133150~piPK:64133175~theSiteP K:239419,00.html (accessed April 21, 2009).

6. See note 4.
7. Standard and Poor's, "Company History: Historical Timeline," http://www2
.standardandpoors.com/portal/site/sp/en/us/page.topic/aboutsp_ch/4,2,2,0,0,0,0,
0,0,0,0,0,0,0,0,0.html?lid=us_topnav_comphistory (accessed April 21, 2009).
8. Antoine van Agtmael, *The Emerging Markets Century: How a New Breed of
World-Class Companies Is Overtaking the World* (New York City: Free Press,
2007). The previous paragraphs borrowed liberally from van Agtmael's recount-
ing of how the term "emerging markets" was coined.
9. Federal Reserve, "Flows of Funds Report 1974–1985," http://www
.federalreserve.gov/releases/z1/ (accessed April 23, 2009).
10. International Monetary Fund, "World Economic Outlook," (April 2009).
http://www.imf.org/external/pubs/ft/weo/2008/01/weodata/index.aspx (accessed
April 21, 2009). Data are based on the "Emerging and developing economies"
category as defined by the IMF.
11. See note 4; Thomson Datastream.
12. See note 10; Data are based on the "Emerging and developing economies" category as defined by the IMF.
13. See note 4; Thomson Datastream.
14. Ibid.
15. See note 4.
16. See note 4; Thomson Datastream.

CHAPTER 2: LIONS, TIGERS & DRAGONS, OH MY!

1. The World Bank Group, *The East Asian Miracle: Economic Growth and Public
Policy* (Oxford University Press, 1993). Not all of the countries listed by the
World Bank are formally considered emerging markets by MSCI today. For
instance, Hong Kong and Singapore are classified as developed markets.
2. The World Bank Group, "World Development Indicators," http://web
.worldbank.org/WBSITE/EXTERNAL/DATASTATISTICS/0,,contentMDK:
20398986~menuPK:64133163~pagePK:64133150~piPK:64133175~theSiteP
K:239419,00.html (accessed April 21, 2009).
3. Emerging Asia equities are defined as those countries in the MSCI Emerging
Asia Index as of 12/31/07.
4. Source: MSCI. The MSCI information may only be used for your internal use,
may not be reproduced or redisseminated in any form and may not be used to
create any financial instruments or products or any indices. The MSCI
information is provided on an "as is" basis, and the user of this information
assumes the entire risk of any use made of this information. MSCI, each of
its affiliates and each other person involved in or related to compiling, computing, or creating any MSCI information (collectively, the "MSCI Parties")
expressly disclaims all warranties (including, without limitation, any warranties
of originality, accuracy, completeness, timeliness, non-infringement, merchantability, and fitness for a particular purpose) with respect to this information.

Without limiting any of the foregoing, in no event shall any MSCI Party have any liability for any direct, indirect, special, incidental, punitive, consequential (including, without limitation, lost profits), or any other damages.

5. See note 1.
6. International Monetary Fund, "World Economic Outlook," (April 2009); See note 4; Inflation rates from the IMF were averaged across emerging market countries as defined by MSCI for the time period 1984–1995.
7. See note 1.
8. Paul Krugman, "The Myth of Asia's Miracle," *Foreign Affairs* 73 (Nov/Dec 1994), 62.
9. Bloomberg Financial, L.P., as of August 31, 2009.
10. Federal Reserve Bank of San Francisco, "What Caused East Asia's Financial Crisis?" (August 7, 1998), 98-24.
11. Public Broadcasting Service, "Timeline of the Panic," http://www.pbs.org/wgbh/pages/frontline/shows/crash/etc/cron.html (accessed April 21, 2009).
12. Ibid.
13. See note 4; Thomson Datastream.
14. See note 4.
15. For a thorough analysis of these phenomenon, see Charles P. Kindleberger's classic *Manias, Panics, and Crashes: A History of Financial Crisis*, now in its fifth edition.
16. Robert Shiller, *Irrational Exuberance* (Broadway Business 2nd Edition, 2006), 85.
17. "Market Crashes: The South Sea Bubble," *Investopedia,* http://www.investopedia.com/features/crashes/crashes3.asp (accessed April 21, 2009).
18. Sonthya Vanichavatana, "Thailand Real Estate Market Cycles: Case Study of 1997 Economic Crisis," *General Housing Bank* 1, Issue 1 (June–December 2007).
19. Sebastian Edwards and Jeffrey Frankel, *Preventing Currency Crisis in Emerging Markets* (University of Chicago Press, 2002).
20. Ibid.
21. Don Kirk, "G.M. to Offer Formal Plan for Takeover of Daewoo," *New York Times* (May 30, 2001), http://query.nytimes.com/gst/fullpage.html?res=990CE0DB123CF933A05756C0A9679C8B63&n=Top%2FReference%2FTimes%20Topics%2FSubjects%2FC%2FCorporations (accessed April 23, 2009).
22. International Monetary Fund, "The IMF's Response to the Asian Crisis," (January 1999), http://www.imf.org/external/np/exr/facts/asia.htm (accessed April 23, 2009).
23. Michael Shari, "The IMF Bailout: Up In Smoke," *Business Week* (May 21, 1998), http://www.businessweek.com/1998/22/b3580019.htm (accessed April 23, 2009).
24. For an exhaustive account of Mao's rise to power and nearly 30-year reign see *Mao: The Unknown Story* by Jung Chang and Jon Halliday.
25. IMF World Economic Outlook Database, October 2008.

26. James Kynge, *China Shakes the World: A Titan's Rise and Troubled Future and the Challenge for America* (Mariner Books, 2007).
27. See note 25.
28. Thomson Datastream.
29. Bloomberg Finance L.P., Thomson Datastream.
30. "Rushing on by Road, Rail and Air," *The Economist* (February 14, 2008), http://www.economist.com/world/asia/displaystory.cfm?story_id=10697210 (accessed April 23, 2009).
31. See note 28.
32. Global Financial Data.
33. See note 25.
34. Bloomberg Finance L.P., Fisher Investments research.
35. Tan Kong Yam, "Holding Out For China Share Reform Benefits," FT Mandate (December 2005), http://www.ftmandate.com/news/fullstory.php/aid/937/Holding_out_for_china_share_reform_benefits.html (accessed April 23, 2009).
36. Geoff Dyer, "PetroChina Fuelling China's Share Boom," *Financial Times* (November 5, 2007), http://www.ft.com/cms/s/0/258436ac-8bc3-11dc-af4d-0000779fd2ac.html (accessed April 23, 2009).
37. "A Record Year for Chinese IPOs," *Reuters* (January 23, 2008), http://www.reuters.com/article/pressRelease/idUS137538+23-Jan-2008+PRN20080123?bcsi_scan_408DE456E3075246=0tGa+T9qHB6TON P3Hr1uSCEAAADCuM8D (accessed April 23, 2009).
38. Chi-Chu Tschang, "China's Great Railway Expansion," *BusinessWeek* (October 23, 2008), http://www.businessweek.com/magazine/content/08_44/b4106067132043.htm (accessed April 23, 2009).

CHAPTER 3: LATIN AMERICA AND THE VAGARIES OF BOOM AND BUST

1. Henry M. Littlefield, "The Wizard of Oz: Parable on Populism," *American Quarterly*, 16, 1. (1964), 47–58.
2. Edwin Williamson, *The Penguin History of Latin America*, (Penguin Books, 1992), 347–348.
3. "Research Tools: Economics A-Z," *The Economist*, http://www.economist.com/research/Economics/alphabetic.cfm?letter=G#ginicoefficient (accessed April 24, 2009). Ranking based on the UN's Gini Coefficient.
4. Milton Friedman and Anna Jacobson Schwartz, *A Monetary History of the United States 1867–1960* (Princeton University Press, 1971).
5. IMF World Economic Outlook Databases, October 2008.
6. "A Stimulating Question," *The Economist* (December 11, 2008), http://www.economist.com/finance/displaystory.cfm?story_id=12775548 (accessed April 24, 2009).

7. Source: MSCI. The MSCI information may only be used for your internal use, may not be reproduced or redisseminated in any form and may not be used to create any financial instruments or products or any indices. The MSCI information is provided on an "as is" basis, and the user of this information assumes the entire risk of any use made of this information. MSCI, each of its affiliates and each other person involved in or related to compiling, computing, or creating any MSCI information (collectively, the "MSCI Parties") expressly disclaims all warranties (including, without limitation, any warranties of originality, accuracy, completeness, timeliness, non-infringement, merchantability, and fitness for a particular purpose) with respect to this information. Without limiting any of the foregoing, in no event shall any MSCI Party have any liability for any direct, indirect, special, incidental, punitive, consequential (including, without limitation, lost profits), or any other damages; Thomson Datastream.

8. The World Bank Group. Represents external debt of Latin American & Caribbean region.

9. See note 2.

10. Energy Information Administration.

11. Thomson Datastream.

12. Ibid.

13. FDIC Division of Research and Statistics,"History of the Eighties—Lessons for the Future," FDIC (December 1997), www.fdic.gov/bank/historical/history (accessed May 4, 2009).

14. Ibid.

15. Michael P. Dooley, *A Retrospective on the Debt Crisis* (National Bureau of Economic Research, 1994), 264.

16. Charles P. Kindleberger and Robert Z. Aliber, *Manias, Panics, and Crashes* (John Wiley & Sons, 2005), 4.

17. See note 13.

18. Ibid.

19. Global Financial Data.

20. Ibid.

21. See note 13.

22. Manuel Monteagudo, "The Debt Problem: The Baker Plan and the Brady Initiative," in *La Dette Extérieure: The External Debt* (Martinus Nijhoff Publishers, 1995), 141.

23. Ian Vázquez, "The Brady Plan and Market-Based Solutions to Debt Crisis," *The Cato Journal 16*, 2.

24. Ibid.

25. IMF World Economic Outlook Database, October 2008.

26. Garciela L. Kaminsky and Alfredo Pereira, "The Debt Crisis: Lessons of the 1980s for the 1990s,"*Journal of Development Economics* 50, 1 (1996).

27. World Bank Group.

28. See note 2.
29. Scott Gavin and Anastasia Toufexis, "Brazil Victory for the 'Great Conciliator'," *Time* (January 28, 1985), http://www.time.com/time/magazine/article/0,9171,959258,00.html (accessed April 28, 2009).
30. See note 2.
31. Ibid.
32. Ibid.
33. See note 25.
34. Global Financial Data.
35. Paul Krugman, *The Return of Depression Economics* (W.W. Norton and Company, 2000), 42.
36. See note 25.
37. Huw Pill, *Mexico: The Tequila Crisis 1994–95* (Harvard Business School Publishing), 38, See note 35.
39. See note 37.
40. See note 34.
41. See note 35.
42. See note 37.
43. See note 34.
44. See note 37.
45. See note 35.

CHAPTER 4: FROM THE RUBLE OF THE IRON CURTAIN TO THE LEGACY OF THE APARTHEID

1. Michael J. Economides and Donna Marie D'Aleo, *From Soviet to Putin and Back* (Energy Tribune Publishing, 2008), 322.
2. Ibid.
3. Ibid.
4. Ibid.
5. Ibid.
6. Ibid.
7. Ibid.
8. Ibid.
9. Ibid.
10. Ibid.
11. IMF World Economic Outlook Database, October 2008.
12. See note 1.
13. Ibid.
14. Ibid.
15. David Hoffman, *The Oligarchs: Wealth and Power in the New Russia* (PublicAffairs, 2003), 362.
16. See note 1.

17. Ibid.
18. Energy Information Administration.
19. Source: MSCI. The MSCI information may only be used for your internal use, may not be reproduced or redisseminated in any form and may not be used to create any financial instruments or products or any indices. The MSCI information is provided on an "as is" basis and the user of this information assumes the entire risk of any use made of this information. MSCI, each of its affiliates and each other person involved in or related to compiling, computing or creating any MSCI information (collectively, the "MSCI Parties") expressly disclaims all warranties (including, without limitation, any warranties of originality, accuracy, completeness, timeliness, non-infringement, merchantability and fitness for a particular purpose) with respect to this information. Without limiting any of the foregoing, in no event shall any MSCI Party have any liability for any direct, indirect, special, incidental, punitive, consequential (including, without limitation, lost profits) or any other damages; Thomson Datastream.
20. See note 15.
21. Global Financial Data (RTS Index).
22. John Odling-Smee, *The IMF and Russia in the 1990s*, IMF Working Paper (August 2004), 21.
23. Abbigail J. Chiodo and Michael T. Owyang. *A Case Study of a Currency Crisis: The Russian Default of 1998*, (The Federal Reserve Bank of St. Louis, November/December 2002).
24. See note 15.
25. See note 21.
26. Global Financial Data.
27. See note 15.
28. "Russia: Fears of a New Ruble Crisis," Stratfor Global Intelligence (January 7, 2009), http://www.stratfor.com/analysis/20090106_russia_fears_new_ruble_crisis (accessed May 7, 2009).
29. See note 21.
30. See note 11.
31. See note 1.
32. "Putin Clinches Rusian Presidency," *BBC News* (March 27, 2000), http://news.bbc.co.uk/2/hi/europe/692001.stm (accessed April 28, 2009).
33. See note 11.
34. See note 1.
35. Ibid.
36. Ibid.
37. Andrew Kramer, "Last Piece of Russian Oil Giant is Sold," *New York Times* (May 12, 2007), http://www.nytimes.com/2007/05/12/business/worldbusiness/12yukos.html?_r=1 (accessed April 28, 2009).
38. "Sergei Pulls It Off," *The Economist* (July 20, 2006), http://www.economist.com/finance/displaystory.cfm?story_id=E1_STJRSNV (accessed April 28, 2009).

39. Eric P. Louw, *The Rise, Fall, and Legacy of Apartheid* (Greenwood Publishing Group, 2004).
40. Stephen R. Lewis, *The Economics of Apartheid* (Council on Foreign Relations, 1990), 14–15.
41. Ibid.
42. Chamber of Mines of South Africa.
43. South African Reserve Bank, *Quarterly Bulletin.*
44. Alan Hirsch, *Season of Hope* (University of KwaZulu-Natal Press, 2005), 2.
45. Bloomberg Financial L.P.
46. See note 44.
47. "South Africa's Jumbos Head North," *Economist* (December 10, 1998).
48. "Broad-Based Black Economic Empowerment Strategy & Codes of Good Practice to Broad-Based Black Economic Empowerment," Department of Trade and Industry, http://www.dti.gov.za/ (accessed May 7, 2009).
49. Rebecca Bream and Alec Russell, "Anglo in Empowerment Deal," *Financial Times* (September 5, 2007), http://www.ft.com/cms/s/0/39619d58-5b4a-11dc -8c32-0000779fd2ac.html (accessed April 28, 2009).
50. "The Way to BEE," *Economist* (December 19, 2006), http://www.economist.com/ business/displaystory.cfm?story_id=E1_RQVDTDN (accessed April 28, 2009).
51. Luke Peterson and Alan Beattie, "Mining Trio Mount Court Challenge to South Africa," *Financial Times* (March 9, 2007), http://www.ft.com/cms/s/0/ d4e0c0a6-cde2-11db-839d-000b5df10621.html (accessed April 28, 2009).

CHAPTER 5: FROM THE PAST TO TODAY—HOW TO APPROACH EMERGING MARKETS

1. Thomson Datastream; Source: MSCI. The MSCI information may only be used for your internal use, may not be reproduced or redisseminated in any form and may not be used to create any financial instruments or products or any indices. The MSCI information is provided on an "as is" basis, and the user of this information assumes the entire risk of any use made of this information. MSCI, each of its affiliates and each other person involved in or related to compiling, computing, or creating any MSCI information (collectively, the "MSCI Parties") expressly disclaims all warranties (including, without limitation, any warranties of originality, accuracy, completeness, time-liness, non-infringement, merchantability, and fitness for a particular purpose) with respect to this information. Without limiting any of the foregoing, in no event shall any MSCI Party have any liability for any direct, indirect, special, incidental, punitive, consequential (including, without limitation, lost profits), or any other damages.
2. Ibid.
3. Source: MSCI. The MSCI information may only be used for your internal use, may not be reproduced or redisseminated in any form and may not be

used to create any financial instruments or products or any indices. The MSCI information is provided on an "as is" basis, and the user of this information assumes the entire risk of any use made of this information. MSCI, each of its affiliates and each other person involved in or related to compiling, computing, or creating any MSCI information (collectively, the "MSCI Parties") expressly disclaims all warranties (including, without limitation, any warranties of originality, accuracy, completeness, timeliness, non-infringement, merchantability, and fitness for a particular purpose) with respect to this information. Without limiting any of the foregoing, in no event shall any MSCI Party have any liability for any direct, indirect, special, incidental, punitive, consequential (including, without limitation, lost profits), or any other damages.

4. Ibid.
5. Ibid.
6. See note 1.
7. See note 3.
8. Ibid.
9. Ibid.
10. See note 1.
11. See note 3.
12. Ibid.
13. Ibid.
14. Gary P. Brinson, Brian D. Singer, and Gilbert L. Beebower, "Determinants of Portfolio Performance II: An Update," *Financial Analysts Journal 47* (1991), 40–48.
15. As measured by MSCI Taiwan, as of 12/31/2008; see note 3.

CHAPTER 6: DEVELOPING PORTFOLIO DRIVERS

1. Thomson Datastream, Source: MSCI. The MSCI information may only be used for your internal use, may not be reproduced or redisseminated in any form and may not be used to create any financial instruments or products or any indices. The MSCI information is provided on an "as is" basis, and the user of this information assumes the entire risk of any use made of this information. MSCI, each of its affiliates and each other person involved in or related to compiling, computing, or creating any MSCI information (collectively, the "MSCI Parties") expressly disclaims all warranties (including, without limitation, any warranties of originality, accuracy, completeness, timeliness, non-infringement, merchantability, and fitness for a particular purpose) with respect to this information. Without limiting any of the foregoing, in no event shall any MSCI Party have any liability for any direct, indirect, special, incidental, punitive, consequential (including, without limitation, lost profits), or any other damages.
2. Ibid.
3. Ibid.

4. Associated Press, "Raw Data: List of Recent Coups in Thailand's History," *Fox News* (September 19, 2006), http://www.foxnews.com/story/0,2933,214562,00 .html (accessed April 28, 2009).
5. International Monetary Fund, World Economic Outlook Database, October 2008.
6. See note 1.
7. Global Financial Data, Brazil's currency devalued in 1986, 1989, 1990, 1993, and 1994.
8. Jorn Madslien, "Brazil's Looming Economic Crisis," *BBC News* (August 5, 2002), http://news.bbc.co.uk/1/hi/business/2173296.stm (accessed April 28, 2009).
9. "Lula Wins Brazil Pension Reforms," *BBC News* (December 12, 2003), http:// news.bbc.co.uk/2/hi/americas/3312175.stm (accessed April 28, 2009).
10. Central Bank of Brazil.
11. See note 1.
12. "World Crude Steel Production, 1950 to 2006," International Iron and Steel Institute, http://www.worldsteel.org/?action=storypages&id=193 (accessed July 16, 2008); Metal Producing & Processing Staff, "Global Steel Ouput Rose 7.5% in 2007," *Metal Producing & Processing* (January 24, 2008).
13. Thomson Datastream; as measured by West Texas Intermediate crude oil.
14. US Department of the Interior, "Iron Ore Statistics and Information," *US Geological Survey* (April 2, 2009), http://minerals.usgs.gov/minerals/pubs/ commodity/iron_ore/ (accessed April 28, 2009).
15. See note 1.
16. International Monetary Fund, World Economic Outlook Database, October 2008; See note 1.
17. See note 1.
18. Ibid.
19. Ibid.
20. Ibid.
21. "South Korea in Plan to Attract Capital," *New York Times* (July 8, 2002), http:// www.nytimes.com/2002/07/08/business/south-korea-in-plan-to-attract-capital .html (accessed April 28, 2009).
22. Nicholas Varchaver, "What Warren Thinks...," *Fortune Magazine* (April 14, 2008), http://money.cnn.com/2008/04/11/news/newsmakers/varchaver_ buffett.fortune/index.htm (accessed April 28, 2009).
23. Jude Webber, "IMF Asks Argentina to Clarify Inflation Figures," *Financial Times* (February 11, 2008), http://www.ft.com/cms/s/0/292718a6-d8d5-11dc -8b22-0000779 fd2ac.html (accessed April 28, 2009).

CHAPTER 8: PUTTING IT TOGETHER

1. Bloomberg Finance L.P.
2. Source: MSCI. The MSCI information may only be used for your internal use, may not be reproduced or redisseminated in any form and may not be

used to create any financial instruments or products or any indices. The MSCI information is provided on an "as is" basis and the user of this information assumes the entire risk of any use made of this information. MSCI, each of its affiliates and each other person involved in or related to compiling, computing or creating any MSCI information (collectively, the "MSCI Parties") expressly disclaims all warranties (including, without limitation, any warranties of originality, accuracy, completeness, timeliness, non-infringement, merchantability and fitness for a particular purpose) with respect to this information. Without limiting any of the foregoing, in no event shall any MSCI Party have any liability for any direct, indirect, special, incidental, punitive, consequential (including, without limitation, lost profits) or any other damages.

3. Ibid.
4. Bogle Financial Markets Research Center, "About John C. Bogle," Vanguard (May 2006), http://www.vanguard.com/bogle_site/bogle_bio.html (accessed April 28, 2009).
5. ProFunds website, www.profunds.com.
6. Bloomberg Financial, L.P. as of 4/21/09.
7. Ibid.
8. Securities and Exchange Board of India, "Securities and Exchange Board of India (Foreign Institutional Investors) Regulations," (November 1995, amended October 30, 2008), http://www.sebi.gov.in/Index.jsp?contentDisp=SubSection&sec_id=5&sub_sec_id=5 (accessed April 28, 2009).
9. Ibid.
10. See note 6, as of 4/22/09.
11. Bloomberg Finance L.P.
12. Peter Drysdale, *Reform and Recovery in East Asia: The Role of the State and Economic Enterprise* (Routledge, 2000), 174.
13. Treasury Malaysia Ministry of Finance, "Statement on the Repatriation of Portfolio Capital," (February 4, 1999), http://www2.treasury.gov.my/index .php?option=com_content&view=article&id=812%3Akenyataan-oleh-yb -menteri-kewangan-i-tun-dato-daim-bin-zainuddin-mengenai-repatriasi-modal-por tfolio&catid=53%3Aucapan&Itemid=251&lang=en (accessed April 28, 2009).
14. See note 2.
15. Ibid.
16. Thomson Datastream; See note 2.

About the Author

Austin B. Fraser is a research analyst at Fisher Investments with a focus on emerging markets and macroeconomic strategy. Prior to joining the firm, he worked at Cambridge Associates in Washington, DC, as a research associate. He graduated from the University of Michigan, Ann Arbor with a BA in history and writes a regular column for MarketMinder.com entitled "Reality Check." Originally from Detroit, Michigan, he now resides in San Francisco.

Index